Bailey

SHAKESPEARE

MUCH ADO
ABOUT NOTHING

NOTES

COLES EDITORIAL BOARD

D1115986

ABOUT COLES NOTES

COLES NOTES have been an indispensible aid to students on five continents since 1948.

COLES NOTES are available for a wide range of individual literary works. Clear, concise explanations and insights are provided along with interesting interpretations and evaluations.

Proper use of COLES NOTES will allow the student to pay greater attention to lectures and spend less time taking notes. This will result in a broader understanding of the work being studied and will free the student for increased participation in discussions.

COLES NOTES are an invaluable aid for review and exam preparation as well as an invitation to explore different interpretive paths.

COLES NOTES are written by experts in their fields. It should be noted that any literary judgement expressed herein is just that – the judgement of one school of thought. Interpretations that diverge from, or totally disagree with any criticism may be equally valid.

COLES NOTES are designed to supplement the text and are not intended as a substitute for reading the text itself. Use of the NOTES will serve not only to clarify the work being studied, but should enhance the readers enjoyment of the topic.

ISBN 0-7740-3772-5

Copyright 2009 and Published by
Coles Publishing
A division of Prospero Books
Toronto Canada
Publisher: Indigo Books and Music Inc.

Designed and Printed in Canada

Printed on Legacy Book Opaque 100%, manufactured from 100% post-consumer waste and is FSC-certified.
Manufacturing this book in Canada ensures compliance with strict environmental practices and eliminates the need for international freight shipping, a major contributor to global air pollution.

ANCIENT FOREST FRIENDLY

3 trees were saved for our forests

Preserving our environment
Indigo Books.Gifts.Life chose to use recycled paper for all print editions of this book and saved these resources[1]:

energy	water	greenhouse gases	solid waste
3 million BTUs	2,956 L	74 kg	21 kg

Printed by **Webcom Inc.** on Legacy Book Opaque 100% post-consumer waste.

FSC

Recycled
Supporting responsible use of forest resources

Cert no. SW-COC-002358
www.fsc.org
© 1996 Forest Stewardship Council

[1]Estimates were made using the Environmental Defense Paper Calculator.

Manufacturing this book in Canada ensures compliance with strict environmental practices and eliminates the need for international freight, which is a major contributor to global air pollution

CONTENTS

WILLIAM SHAKESPEARE
LIFE AND WORKS
Biographical Sketch

With the epithet "Dear Son of Memory", Milton praised Shakespeare as one constantly in our memories and brother of the Muses. Certainly no other author has held such sway over the literary world, undiminished through some three and a half centuries of shifting artistic tastes. Shakespeare's plots and his characters have continued to be a living reality for us; as his well known contemporary Ben Jonson wrote, in a familiar tribute, "Thou . . . art alive still, while thy Booke doth live,/ And we have wits to read, and praise to give."

The Early Years

Despite such acclaim and the scholarship it has spawned, our knowledge of Shakespeare's life is sketchy, filled with more questions than answers, even after we prune away the misinformation accumulated over the years. He was baptized on April 26, 1564, in Holy Trinity Church, Stratford-on-Avon. As it was customary to baptize children a few days after birth, we conjecture that he was born on April 23. The monument erected in Stratford states that he died on April 23, 1616, in his fifty-third year.

William was the third child of John Shakespeare, who came to Stratford from Snitterfield before 1532 as a "whyttawer" (tanner) and glover, and Mary Arden, daughter of a wealthy "gentleman of worship" from Wilmecote. They married around 1557. Since John Shakespeare owned one house on Greenhill Street and two on Henley Street, we cannot be certain where William was born, though the Henley Street shrine draws many tourists each year. William's two older sisters died in infancy, but three brothers and two other sisters survived at least into childhood.

Shakespeare's father was fairly well-to-do, dealing in farm products and wool, and owning considerable property in Stratford. After holding a series of minor municipal offices he was elected alderman in 1565, high bailiff (roughly similar to the mayor of today) in 1568, and chief alderman in 1571. There are no records of young Will Shakespeare's education (though there are many unfounded legends), but he undoubtedly attended the town school maintained by the burgesses, which prepared its students for the universities. Ben Jonson's line about Shakespeare's having "small *Latine*, and lesse *Greeke*" refers not to his education but to his lack of indebtedness to the classical writers and dramatists.

On November 27, 1582, a licence to marry was issued to "Willelmum Shaxpere *et* Annam Whateley *de* Temple Grafton," and on

1

the next day a marriage bond for "Willm Shagspere" and "Anne Hathwey of Stratford" was signed by Fulk Sandells and John Richardson, farmers of Stratford. This bond stated that there was no "lawful let or impediment by reason of any precontract, consanguinity, affinity, or by any other lawful means whatsoever"; thus "William and Anne (were) to be married together with once asking of the banns of matrimony." The problem of Anne Whateley has led many researchers and some detractors to argue all kinds of improbabilities, such as the existence of two different Shakespeares and the forging of documents to conceal Shakespeare's true identity. The actual explanation seems to be simple: the clerk who made the marriage licence entry apparently copied the name "Whateley" from a preceding entry, as a glance at the full sheet suggests. (Incidentally, Nicholas Rowe in his life of Shakespeare, published in 1709, well before the discovery of these marriage records, gave Anne's name as Hathaway.) The problems of marriage with Anne Hathaway — he was eighteen and she was twenty-six — and of the bond have caused similar consternation. Why did these two marry when there was such a discrepancy of age? Why only one saying of the banns (rather than the usual three)? Why the emphasis on a possible legal impediment? The answer here is not simple or definite, but the birth of a daughter Susanna, baptized at Holy Trinity on May 26, 1583, seems to explain the odd circumstances. It should be recognized, however, that an engagement to marry was considered legally binding in those days (we still have breach-of-promise suits today) and that premarital relations were not unusual or frowned upon when an engagement had taken place. The circumstances already mentioned, Shakespeare's ensuing activities, and his will bequeathing to Anne "my second best bed with the furniture" have suggested to some that their marriage was not entirely happy. Their other children, the twins Hamnet and Judith, were christened on February 2, 1585.

Theatrical Life

Shakespeare's years before and immediately after the time of his marriage are not charted, but rumor has him as an apprentice to a master butcher or as a country teacher or an actor with some provincial company. He is supposed to have run away from whatever he was doing for livelihood and to have gone to London, where he soon attached himself to some theatrical group. At this time there were only two professional houses established in the London environs, The Theatre (opened in 1576) and The Curtain (opened in 1577). His first connection with the theater was reputedly as holder of horses; that is, one of the stage crew, but a most inferior assignment. Thereafter he became an actor (perhaps at this time he met Ben Jonson), a writer, and a director. Such experience had its mark in the theatricality of his plays. We do know that he was established in London by 1592, when Robert Greene lamented in *A Groatsworth of Wit* (September, 1592) that professional actors had gained priority in the theater over university-trained writers like himself: "There is an upstart Crow, beautified with our feathers, that with his *Tygers hart wrapt in a Players hyde*, supposes he is as well able to bombast out a lanke verse as the best of you: and beeing an absolute *Iohannes fac totum* (Jack-of-all-trades), is in his owne conceit the onely Shake-scene in a countrey." An apology for Greene's ill-humored statement by Henry Chettle, the editor of the pamphlet, appeared around December 1592 in *Kind-Hart's Dream*.

Family Affairs

To return to the known details of family life, Shakespeare's son Hamnet was buried at Stratford on August 11, 1596; his father was given a coat of arms on October 20, 1596; and he purchased New Place (a refurbished tourist attraction today) on May 4, 1597. The London playwright obviously had not severed connections with his birthplace, and he was reflecting his new affluence by being known as William Shakespeare of Stratford-upon-Avon, in the County of Warwick, Gentleman. His father was buried in Stratford on September 8, 1601; his mother, on September 9, 1608. His daughter Susanna married Dr. John Hall on June 5, 1607, and they had a child named Elizabeth. His other daughter, Judith, married Thomas Quiney on February 10, 1616, without special licence, during Lent and was thus excommunicated. Shakespeare revised his will on March 25, 1616, and was buried on April 25, 1616 (according to the parish register). A monument by Gerard Janssen was erected in the Holy Trinity chancel in 1623 but many, like Milton several years later, protested:

> What needs my *Shakespeare* for his honour'd Bones,
> The labour of an age in piled Stone, . . .
> Thou in our wonder and astonishment
> Hast built thy self a live-long Monument.

Shakespeare's Writings

Order of Appearance

Dating of Shakespeare's early plays, while based on inconclusive evidence, has tended to hover around the early 1590's. Almost certainly it is his chronicles of Henry the Sixth that Philip Henslowe, an important theatrical manager of the day, referred to in his diary as being performed during March-May, 1592. An allusion to these plays also occurs in Thomas Nashe's *Piers Penniless His Supplication to the Devil* (August, 1592). Greene's quotation about a tiger is a paraphrase of "O tiger's heart wrapt in a woman's hide" from *Henry VI*, Part III.

The first published work to come from Shakespeare's hand was *Venus and Adonis* (1593), a long stanzaic poem, dedicated to Henry

Wriothesley, Earl of Southampton. A year later *The Rape of Lucrece* appeared, also dedicated to Southampton. Perhaps poetry was pursued during these years because the London theaters were closed as a result of a virulent siege of plague. The *Sonnets*, published in 1609, may owe something to Southampton, who had become Shakespeare's patron. Perhaps some were written as early as the first few years of the 1590's. They were mentioned (along with a number of plays) in 1598 by Francis Meres in his *Palladis Tamia*, and sonnets 138 and 144 were printed without authority by William Jaggard in *The Passionate Pilgrim* (1599).

There is a record of a performance of *A Comedy of Errors* at Gray's Inn (one of the law colleges) on December 28, 1594, and, during early 1595, Shakespeare was paid, along with the famous actors Richard Burbage and William Kempe, for performances before the Queen by the Lord Chamberlain's Men, a theatrical company formed the year before. The company founded the Globe Theatre on the south side of the Thames in 1599 and became the King's Men when James ascended the throne. Records show frequent payments to the company through its general manager John Heminge. From 1595 through 1614 there are numerous references to real estate transactions and other legal matters, to many performances, and to various publications connected with Shakespeare.

Order of Publication

The first plays to be printed were *Titus Andronicus* around February, 1594, and the garbled versions of *Henry VI*, Parts II and III in 1594. (Some scholars, however, question whether the last two are versions of *Henry VI*, Parts II and III, and some dispute Shakespeare's authorship.) Thereafter *Richard III* appeared in 1597 and 1598; *Richard II*, in 1597 and twice in 1598; *Romeo and Juliet*, in 1597 (a pirated edition) and 1599, and many others. Some of the plays appear in individual editions, with or without Shakespeare's name on the title page, but eighteen are known only from their appearance in the first collected volume (the so-called First Folio) of 1623. The editors were Heminge and Henry Condell, another member of Shakespeare's company. *Pericles* was omitted from the First Folio although it had appeared in 1609, 1611, and 1619; it was added to the Third Folio in 1664.

There was reluctance to publish plays at this time for various reasons; many plays were carelessly written for fast production; collaboration was frequent; plays were not really considered *reading* matter; they were sometimes circulated in manuscript; and the theatrical company, not the author, owned the rights. Those plays given individual publication appeared in a quarto, so named from the size of the page. A single sheet of paper was folded twice to make four leaves (thus *quarto*) or eight pages; these four leaves constitute one signature (one section of a bound book). A page measures about 6¾ in. x 8½ in. On the other hand, a folio sheet is folded once to make two leaves or four pages; three sheets, or twelve pages, constitute a signature. The page is approximately 8½ in. x 13¾ in.

Authorized publication occurred when a company disbanded, when money was needed but rights were to be retained, when a play failed or ran into licensing difficulties (thus, hopefully, the printed work would justify the play against the criticism), or when a play had been pirated. Authorized editions are called good quartos. Piratical publication might occur when the manuscript of a play had circulated privately, when a member of a company desired money for himself, or when a stenographer or memorizer took the play down in the theater (such a version was recognizable by inclusion of stage directions derived from an eyewitness, by garbled sections, etc.). Pirated editions are called bad quartos; there are at least five bad quartos of Shakespeare's plays.

Authenticity of Works

Usually thirty-seven plays are printed in modern collections of Shakespeare's works but some recent scholars have urged the addition of two more: *Edward III* and *Two Noble Kinsmen*. A case has also been advanced, unconvincingly, for a fragment of the play on Sir Thomas More. At times, six of the generally-accepted plays have been questioned: *Henry VI*, Parts I, II and III, *Timon of Athens*, *Pericles* and *Henry VIII*. The first four are usually accepted today (one hopes all question concerning *Timon* has finally ended), but if Shakespeare did not write these plays in their entirety, he certainly wrote parts of them. Of course, collaboration in those days was commonplace. Aside from the two long narrative poems already mentioned and the sonnets (Nos. 1-152, but not Nos. 153-154), Shakespeare's poetic output is uncertain. *The Passionate Pilgrim* (1599) contains only five authenticated poems (two sonnets and three verses from *Love's Labour's Lost*); *The Phoenix and the Turtle* (1601) may be his, but the authenticity of *A Lover's Complaint* (appended to the sonnets) is highly questionable.

Who Was Shakespeare?

At this point we might mention a problem that has plagued Shakespeare study for over a century: who was Shakespeare? Those who would like to make the author of the plays someone else — Francis Bacon or the Earl of Oxford or even Christopher Marlowe (dead long before most of the plays were written) — have used the lack of information of Shakespeare's early years and the confusion in the evidence we have been examining to advance their candidate. But the major arguments against Shakespeare show the source of these speculators' disbelief to be in classconscious snobbery and perhaps in a perverse adherence to minority opinion. The most common argument is that no one of Shakespeare's background, lack of education, and lack of aristocratic experience could know all that the author knew. But study will reveal that such information was readily available in various popular sources, that some of it lies in the literary sources used for the play, and that Shakespeare was probably not totally lacking in education or in social decorum. The more significant question of style and tone is not dealt with — nor could it successfully be raised. Bacon, for example, no matter how much we admire his mind and his writings, exhibits a writing style diametrically opposite to Shakespeare's, a style most unpoetic and often flat. The student would be wise not to waste time rehashing these unfounded theories. No such question was raised in the seventeenth or eighteenth centuries, and no serious student of the plays today doubts that Shakespeare *was* Shakespeare.

Shakespeare's Plays

Exact dates for Shakespeare's plays remain a source of debate among scholars. The following serve only as a general frame of reference.

	COMEDIES	TRAGEDIES	HISTORIES
1591			Henry VI, Part I
1592	Comedy of Errors		Henry VI, Part II
1592	Two Gentlemen of Verona		Henry VI, Part III
1593	Love's Labour's Lost	Titus Andronicus	Richard III
1594			King John
1595	Midsummer Night's Dream	Romeo and Juliet	Richard II
1596	Merchant of Venice		
1596	Taming of the Shrew		
1597			Henry IV, Part I
1598	Much Ado About Nothing		Henry IV, Part II
1599	As You Like It	Julius Caesar	
1599	Merry Wives of Windsor		Henry V
1601	Twelfth Night	Hamlet	
1602	Troilus and Cressida		
1602	All's Well That Ends Well		
1604	Measure for Measure	Othello	
1605		King Lear	
1606		Macbeth	
1607		Timon of Athens	
1607		Antony and Cleopatra	
1608	Pericles		
1609		Coriolanus	
1610	Cymbeline		
1611	Winter's Tale		
1611	Tempest		
1613			Henry VIII

Shakespeare's England

The world of Elizabethan and Jacobean England was a world of growth and change. The great increase in the middle class, and in the population as a whole, demanded a new economy and means of livelihood, a new instrument of government (one recognizing "rights" and changed class structure), a new social code and a broad base of entertainment. The invention of printing a century before had contributed to that broader base, but it was the theater that supplied the more immediate needs of the greatest numbers. The theater grew and along with it came less-educated, more money-conscious writers, who gave the people what they wanted: entertainment. But Shakespeare, having passed through a brief period of hack writing, proceeded to set down important ideas in memorable language throughout most of his career. His plays, particularly the later ones, have been analyzed by recent critics in terms of literary quality through their metaphor, verse-line, relationships with psychology and myth, and elaborate structure. Yet Shakespeare was a man of the stage, and the plays were written to be performed. Only this will fully account for the humor of a deadly serious play like *Hamlet* or the spectacle of a *Coriolanus*.

Life in London

During Shakespeare's early years there, London was a walled city of about 200,000, with seven gates providing access to the city from the east, north, and west. It was geographically small and crisscrossed by narrow little streets and lanes. The various wards each had a parish church that dominated the life of the close-knit community. To the south and outside were slums and the haunts of criminal types, and farther out were the agricultural lands and huge estates. As the population increased and the central area declined, the fashionable people of the city moved toward the west, where the palace of Westminster lay. Houses were generally rented out floor by floor and sometimes room by room. Slums were common within the city, too, though close to pleasant enough streets and squares. "Merrie Olde England" was not really clean, nor were its people, for in those days there were no sewers or drains except the gutter in the middle of the street, into which garbage would be emptied to be floated off by the rain to Fleet ditch or Moor ditch. Plague was particularly ravaging in 1592, 1593-94 (when the theaters were closed to avoid contamination) and 1603. Medical knowledge, of course, was slight; ills were "cured" by amputation, leeching, blood-letting and cathartics. The city was (and still is) dominated by St. Paul's Cathedral, around which booksellers clustered on Paternoster Row.

Religious Atmosphere

Of great significance for the times was religion. Under Elizabeth, a state church had developed; it was Protestant in nature and was called Anglican (or today, Episcopalian) but it had arisen from Henry VIII's break with the Pope and from a compromise with the Roman Catholics who had gained power under Mary Tudor.

The Church of England was headed by the Archbishop of Canter

7

bury, who was to be an increasingly important figure in the early part of the seventeenth century. There were also many schismatic groups, which generally desired further departures from Roman Catholicism. Calvinists were perhaps the most numerous and important of the Protestant groups. The Puritans, who were Calvinist, desired to "purify" the church of ritual and certain dogmas, but during the 1590's they were lampooned as extremists in dress and conduct.

Political Milieu

During Shakespeare's lifetime there were two monarchs: Elizabeth, 1558-1603, and James I, 1603-1625. Elizabeth was the daughter of Henry VIII and Anne Boleyn, his second wife, who was executed in 1536. After Henry's death, his son by his third wife, Jane Seymore (died in 1537), reigned as Edward VI. He was followed by Mary Tudor, daughter of Henry's first wife, Catherine of Aragon. Mary was a Roman Catholic, who tried to put down religious dissension by persecution of both Protestants and Catholics. Nor did her marriage to Philip II of Spain endear her to the people.

Elizabeth's reign was troubled by many offers of marriage, particularly from Spanish and French nobles — all Roman Catholic — and by the people's concern for an heir to the throne. English suitors generally cancelled one another out by intrigue or aggressiveness. One of the most prominent was the Earl of Essex, Robert Devereux, who fell in and out of favor; he apparently attempted to take over the reins of control, only to be captured, imprisoned and executed in February, 1601. One claimant to the throne was Mary of Scotland, a Roman Catholic and widow of Francis II of France. She was the second cousin of Elizabeth, tracing her claim through her grandmother, who was Henry VIII's sister. Finally, settlement came with Elizabeth's acceptance of Mary's son as heir apparent, though Mary was to be captured, tried and executed for treason in 1587. Mary had abdicated the throne of Scotland in 1567 in favor of her son, James VI. His ascent to the throne of England in 1603 as James I joined the two kingdoms for the first time, although Scotland during the seventeenth century often acted independently of England.

Contemporary Events

Political and religious problems were intermingled in the celebrated Gunpowder Plot. Angry over fines that were levied upon those not attending Church of England services — primarily Roman Catholics — and offended by difficulties over papal envoys, a group of Catholics plotted to blow up Parliament, and James with it, at its first session on November 5, 1605. A cache of gunpowder was stored in the cellar, guarded by various conspirators, among them Guy Fawkes. The plot was discovered before it could be carried out and Fawkes, on duty at the time, was apprehended. The execution of the plotters and the triumph of the anti-Papists led in succeeding years to celebrations in the streets and the hanging of Fawkes in effigy.

Among the most noteworthy public events during these times were the wars with the Spanish, which included the defeat of the Spanish Armada in 1588, the battle in the Lowlands in 1590-1594, the expedition to Cadiz under Essex in 1596 and the expedition to the Azores (the Islands Expedition), also under Essex, in 1597. With trading companies especially set up for colonization and exploitation, travel excited the imagination of the people: here was a new way of life, here were new customs brought back by the sailors and merchants, here was a new dream world to explore.

In all, the years from around 1590 to 1601 were trying ones for English people, relieved only by the news from abroad, the new affluence and the hope for the future under James. Writers of the period frequently reflect, however, the disillusionment and sadness of those difficult times.

The Elizabethan Theater

Appearance

The Elizabethan playhouse developed from the medieval inn with its rooms grouped around a courtyard into which a stage was built. This pattern was used in The Theatre, built by James Burbage in 1576: a square frame building (later round or octagonal) with a square yard, three tiers of galleries, each jutting out over the one below, and a stage extending into the middle of the yard, where people stood or sat on improvised seats. There was no cover over the yard or stage and lighting was therefore natural. Thus performances were what we might consider late matinees or early evening performances; in summer, daylight continues in London until around ten o'clock.

Other theaters were constructed during the ensuing years: The Curtain in 1577, The Rose in 1587 (on Bankside), The Swan in 1595 (also Bankside) and Shakespeare's playhouse, The Globe, in 1599 (not far from The Rose). There is still some question about the exact dimensions of this house, but it seems to have been octagonal, each side measuring about 36 feet, with an over-all diameter of 84 feet. It was about 33 feet to the eaves, and the yard was 56 feet in diameter. Three sides were used for backstage and to serve the needs of the players. There was no curtain or proscenium, hence the spectators became part of the action. Obviously, the actors' asides and soliloquies were effective under these conditions.

There was no real scenery and there were only a few major props; thus the lines of the play had to reveal locations and movement, changes in time or place, etc. In this way, too, it was easier to establish a nonrealistic setting, for all settings were created in words. On either side of the stage were doors, within the flooring were trapdoors (for entrances of ghosts, etc.), and behind the main stage was the inner stage or recess. Here, indoor scenes (such as a court or a bedchamber) were played, and some props could be used because the inner stage was usually concealed by a curtain when not in use. It might also have served to hide someone behind the ever-present arras, like Polonius in *Hamlet*. The "chamber" was on the second level, with windows and a balcony. On the third level was another chamber, primarily for musicians.

Actors

An acting company such as the Lord Chamberlain's Men was a fellowship of ten to fifteen sharers with some ten to twelve extras, three or four boys (often to play women's roles) who might become full sharers, and stagehands. There were rival companies, each with its leading dramatist and leading tragic actor and clown. The Lord Admiral's Men, organized in 1594, boasted Ben Jonson and the tragedian Edward Alleyn. Some of the rivalry of this War of the Theaters is reflected in the speeches of Hamlet, who also comments on the ascendancy and unwarranted popularity of the children's companies (like the Children of Blackfriars) in the late 1590's.

The company dramatist, of course, had to think in terms of the members of his company as he wrote his play. He had to make use of the physical features and peculiar talents of the actors, making sure, besides, that there was a role for each member. The fact that women's parts were taken by boys imposed obvious limitations on the range of action. Accordingly, we often find women characters impersonating men; for example, Robert Goffe played Portia in *The Merchant of Venice*, and Portia impersonates a male lawyer in the important trial scene. Goffe also played Juliet, and Anne in *Richard III*, and Oberon in *Midsummer Night's Dream*. The influence of an actor on the playwright can be seen, on the one hand, by noting the "humor" characters portrayed so competently by Thomas Pope, who was a choleric Mercutio in *Romeo*, a melancholic Jaques in *As You Like It*, and a sanguinary Falstaff in *Henry IV*, Part I; and by comparing, on the other hand, the clown Bottom in *Midsummer Night's Dream*, played in a frolicsome manner by William Kempe, with the clown Feste in *Twelfth Night*, sung and danced by Robert Armin. Obviously, too, if a certain kind of character was not available within the company, then that kind of character could not be written into the play. The approach was decidedly different from ours today, where the play almost always comes first and the casting of roles second. The plays were performed in a repertory system, with a different play each afternoon. The average life of a play was about ten performances.

History of the Drama

English drama goes back to native forms developed from playlets presented at Church holidays. Mystery plays dealt with biblical stories such as the Nativity or the Passion, and miracle plays usually depicted the lives of saints. The merchant and craft guilds that came to own and produce the cycles of plays were the forerunners of the theatrical companies of Shakespeare's time. The kind of production these cycles received, either as moving pageants in the streets or as staged shows in a churchyard, influenced the late sixteenth-century production of a secular play: there was an intimacy with the audience and there was a great reliance on words rather than setting and props. Similar involvement with the stage action is experienced by audiences of the arena theater of today.

The morality play, the next form to develop, was an allegory of the spiritual conflict between good and evil in the soul of man. The *dramatis personae* were abstract virtues and vices, with at least one man representing Mankind (or Everyman, as the most popular of these plays was titled). Some modern critics see *Othello* as a kind of morality play in which the soul of Othello is vied for by the aggressively evil Iago (as a kind of Satanic figure) and passively good Desdemona (as a personification of Christian faith in all men). The Tudor interlude — a short, witty, visual play — may have influenced the subplot of the Elizabethan play with its low-life and jesting and visual tricks. In mid-sixteenth century appeared the earliest known English comedies, Nicholas Udall's *Ralph Roister Doister* and *Gammer Gurton's Needle* (of uncertain authorship). Both show the influence of the Roman comic playwright Plautus. Shakespeare's *Comedy of Errors*, performed in the 1590's, was an adaptation of Plautus' *Menaechmi*, both plays featuring twins and an involved story of confused identities. The influence of the Roman tragedian Seneca can be traced from Thomas Norton and Thomas Sackville in *Gorboduc* to *Hamlet*. Senecan tragedy is a tragedy of revenge, characterized by many deaths, much blood-letting, ghosts, feigned madness and the motif of a death for a death.

Shakespeare's Artistry

Plots

Generally, a Shakespearean play has two plots: a main plot and a subplot. The subplot reflects the main plot and is often concerned with inferior characters. Two contrasting examples will suffice: Lear and his daughters furnish the characters for the main plot of filial love and ingratitude, whereas Gloucester and his sons enact the same theme in the subplot; Lear and Gloucester both learn that outward signs of love may be false. In *Midsummer Night's Dream*, the town workmen (Quince, Bottom *et al.*) put on a tragic play in such a hilarious way that it turns the subject of the play — love so strong that the hero will kill himself if his loved one dies first — into farce, but this in the main plot is the "serious" plight of the four mixed-up lovers. In both examples Shakespeare has reinforced his points by subplots dealing with the same subject as the main plot.

Sources

The plots of the Elizabethan plays were usually adapted from other sources. "Originality" was not the sought quality; a kind of variation on a theme was. It was felt that one could better evaluate the playwright's worth by seeing what he did with a familiar tale. What he stressed, how he stressed it, how he restructured the familiar elements — these were the important matters. Shakespeare closely followed Sir Thomas North's very popular translation of Plutarch's *Life of Marcus Antonius*, for example, in writing *Antony and Cleopatra*; and he modified Robert Greene's *Pandosto* and combined it with the Pygmalion myth in *The Winter's Tale*, while drawing the character of Autolycus from certain pamphlets written by Greene. The only plays for which sources have not been clearly determined are *Love's Labour's Lost* (probably based on contemporary events) and *The Tempest* (possibly based on some shipwreck account from travellers to the New World).

Verse and Prose

There is a mixture of verse and prose in the plays, partially because plays fully in verse were out of fashion. Greater variety could thus be achieved and character or atmosphere could be more precisely delineated. Elevated passages, philosophically significant ideas, speeches by men of high rank are in verse, but comic and light parts, speeches including dialect or broken English, and scenes that move more rapidly or simply give mundane information are in prose. The poetry is almost always blank verse (iambic pentameter lines without rhyme). Rhyme is used, however (particularly the couplet), to mark the close of scenes or an important action. Rhyme also serves as a cue for the entrance of another actor or some off-stage business, to point to a change of mood or thought, as a forceful opening after a passage of prose, to convey excitement or passion or sentimentality and to distinguish characters.

Shakespeare's plays may be divided into three general categories, though some plays are not readily classified and further subdivisions may be suggested within a category.

The History Play

The history play, or chronicle, may tend to tragedy, like *Richard II*, or to comedy, like *Henry IV*, Part I. It is a chronicle of some royal personage, often altered for dramatic purposes, even to the point of falsification of the facts. Its popularity may have resulted from the rising of nationalism of the English, nurtured by their successes against the Spanish, their developing trade and colonization, and their rising prestige as a world power. The chronicle was considered a political guide, like the popular *Mirror for Magistrates*, a collection of writings showing what happens when an important leader falls through some error in his ways, his thinking or his personality. Thus the history play counseled the right path by negative, if not positive, means. Accordingly, it is difficult to call *Richard II* a tragedy, since Richard was wrong and his wrongness harmed his people. The political philosophy of Shakespeare's day seemed to favor the view that all usurpation was bad and should be corrected, but not by further usurpation. When that original usurpation had been established, through an heir's ascension to the throne, it was to be accepted. Then any rebellion against the "true" king would be a rebellion against God.

Tragedy

Tragedy in simple terms meant that the protagonist died. Certain concepts drawn from Aristotle's *Poetics* require a tragic hero of high standing, who must oppose some conflicting force, either external or internal. The tragic hero should be dominated by a *hamartia* (a so-called tragic flaw, but really an *excess* of some character trait, e.g., pride, or *hubris*), and it is this *hamartia* that leads to his downfall and, because of his status, to the downfall of others. The action presented in the tragedy must be recognizable to the audience as real and potential: through seeing it enacted, the audience has its passion (primarily suffering) raised, and the conclusion of the action thus brings release from that passion (*catharsis*). A more meaningful way of looking at tragedy in the Elizabethan theater, however, is to see it as that which occurs when essential good (like Hamlet) is wasted (through disaster or death) in the process of driving out evil (such as Claudius represents).

Comedy

Comedy in simple terms meant that the play ended happily for the protagonists. Sometimes the comedy depends on exaggerations of man's eccentricities — comedy of humors; sometimes the comedy is romantic and far-fetched. The romantic comedy was usually based on a mix-up in events or confused identity of characters, particularly by disguise. It moved toward tragedy in that an important person might die and the mix-up might never be unraveled; but in the nick of time something happens or someone appears (sometimes illogically or unexpectedly) and saves the day. It reflects the structure of myth by moving from happiness to despair to resurrection. *The Winter's Tale* is a perfect example of this, for the happiness of the first part is banished with Hermione's exile and Perdita's abandonment; tragedy is near when the lost baby, Perdita, cannot be found and Hermione is presumed dead, but Perdita re-appears, as does Hermione, a statue that suddenly comes to life. Lost identities are established and confusions disappear but the mythic-comic nature of the play is seen in the reuniting of the mother, Hermione, a kind of Ceres, with her daughter, Perdita, a kind of Prosperina. Spring returns, summer will bring the harvest, and the winter of the tale is left behind — for a little while.

What is it, then, that makes Shakespeare's art so great? Perhaps we see in it a whole spectrum of humanity, treated impersonally, but with kindness and understanding. We seldom meet in Shakespeare a weeping philosopher: he may criticize, but he criticizes both sides. After he has done so, he gives the impression of saying, Well, that's the way life is; people will always be like that — don't get upset about it. This is probably the key to the Duke's behavior in *Measure for Measure* — a most unbitter comedy despite former labels. Only in *Hamlet* does Shakespeare not seem to fit this statement; it is the one play that Shakespeare, the person, enters.

As we grow older and our range of experience widens, so, too, does Shakespeare's range seem to expand. Perhaps this lies in the ambiguities of his own materials, which allow for numerous individual readings. We meet our own experiences — and they are ours alone, we think — expressed in phrases that we thought our own or of our own discovery. What makes Shakespeare's art so great, then, is his ability to say so much to so many people in such memorable language: he is himself "the show and gaze o' the time."

MUCH ADO ABOUT NOTHING
Sources and History

The main story of *Much Ado About Nothing* — a young lover is parted from his lady through villainy — dates back to Roman times. However, Shakespeare had a number of fairly contemporary sources that had come down to him through translations and adaptations. Matteo Bandello included the story in his collection entitled *Novelle* (1554), and Belleforest rendered a free translation of the story into French in his *Histoires Tragiques* (1582). Shakespeare also had English sources for the play: Sir John Harington translated Ariosto's *Orlando Furioso* in 1591 (Book V in this work, which somewhat predates Bandello's *Novelle*, contains the Hero-Claudio story); Book II, Canto 4 of Spenser's *The Faerie Queene* (1590) contains the plot; Spenser also introduced the notion of a maid wearing the clothing of her mistress. More recent scholarship has found some additional sources, such as Peter Beverly's *The Historie of Ariodanto and Ieneura* (1565-1566), *The Rock of Regard* (1576) by George Whetstone, and Della Porta's *Gli Duoi Fratelli Rivalli (The Two Rival Brothers)*. The story of Beatrice and Benedick, and the involvement of Dogberry and the watch, are Shakespeare's inventions.

We are not certain when Shakespeare wrote *Much Ado About Nothing*, though evidence seems to point to the years between 1597 and 1600. In *Palladis Tamia* (1598), Francis Meres lists a number of Shakespeare's plays, but excludes *Much Ado*. However, there is conjecture over a play included in the list entitled *Love's Labour's Won*. Since Shakespeare did not write a play by that title, it is thought that Meres called *Much Ado* by that name, for its story demonstrates the opposite of the title of another play, *Love's Labour's Lost*. Shakespeare's acting company registered a copy of *Much Ado* with the only publications licensing bureau at that time. Hence, we find an entry in the *Stationer's Register* in 1600 ordering the play withheld from publication. Apparently the actors were worried that printers would attempt to publish unauthorized editions. Finally the manuscript went to the printer. A rather good quarto edition of the play exists, and Shakespeare's name is on the title page.

The play was immediately successful and acquired a reputation because of Beatrice and Benedick. But, as was the case with other plays by Shakespeare, it was subjected to adaptations and editing by later generations. Sir William D'Avenant created a hybrid in 1662 by combining *Much Ado About Nothing* and *Measure for Measure* (the play was called *The Law Against Lovers*). A minister, James Miller, further destroyed the work by combining D'Avenant's play with *Princess d'Elide*, by Molière, in 1737. Yet the charm of the play has remained constant through the centuries and has earned well-known performers praise for their interpretations of the roles.

Defining the Play

The World of *Much Ado About Nothing*

What did the Elizabethan audience recognize in this play? The answer probably rests with a consideration of the different social levels that made up Shakespeare's audience. Just as *Much Ado* is fragmented into aristocratic, middle-class, and lower-class social levels, so too was Shakespeare's audience. The aristocrats always found something interesting in Shakespeare's plays, and probably assumed that they appreciated the play more than any other class. After all, who but they could understand all those classical references to Europe, Ate, Jove, and Baucis? And they were also familiar with quotes from Thomas Kyd's *The Spanish Tragedy*, as well as from *A Handful of Pleasant Delights*. In Act II, Scene I, Beatrice talks about marriage in terms of dancing, but only the aristocrats would know she was parodying *Orchestra, A Poem of Dancing*, by Sir John Davies. Furthermore, the members of the upper class were no doubt proud of the fact they had actually read the "original" versions of the story. Even though they might have considered Claudio's behavior appalling, the story of Hero and Claudio still must have reminded them strongly of their own literary education: pastorals, romances, sentimental novels, sonnets and love songs. The tradition of conventional courtly behavior that typifies Claudio and Hero was clear to the upper-class members of the audience, who also recognized a certain familiar villainy in Don John, an illegitimate knave whose thoughts are dedicated to the overthrow of a kindly prince. As for the language, how extraordinary they must have thought it to find their glorious English language spoken by a group of lowly players, just as the aristocrats themselves spoke and wrote it at court functions and in their love letters.

On the other hand, the middle-class shopkeepers, bakers, tailors, butchers and brewers, who had taken a day off from work, certainly felt the play must have been written for them alone. Who else would weep so freely at Hero's distress and regret so strongly Claudio's ill-advised, though righteous, anger? And only a father can understand the tribulations of Leonato, the good old man.

The "groundlings" — serving men, water carriers, apprentices — probably appreciated the play far more than anyone. *Much Ado About Nothing* had color, dancing, music, lovely language, counts and princes. The story is good, they probably thought, even though some of the characters are too proud. Dogberry is a very funny fellow because he cannot do anything right, and Don John is even funnier because he is so serious. In short, the play embodied all the beauty, joy and wonder of life that the "groundlings" would probably never experience anywhere else except in the theater.

The World Within *Much Ado About Nothing*

Shakespeare more than adequately painted a picture of courtly romantic love at work, in the story of Hero and Claudio, by placing it in a proper setting of music, dancing, wounded vanity, pride, repentance, and finally, marriage. Yet beyond this, he has put together a little world on a level of society that approaches the "real" world. Observe that all the major characters live in the same house. They go off to a "banquet," a dinner, or a dance; they eavesdrop on each other, play tricks, and are friendly, loving, and angry in turn. They talk to each other like the old friends they apparently are, and the informality of their speech gives us a sense of their spontaneous brilliance and humor. Dogberry asks Leonato to question the "plaintiffs" about a particular person named Deformed, because "the watch heard them/talk of one Deformed." Benedick taunts Claudio about love and marriage and says if he should ever bear the yoke of marriage, "let them signify under my sign 'Here you may see Benedick the married man' " (Act I, Scene 1). At the very end of the play, Don Pedro teases Benedick, who has just kissed Beatrice: "How dost thou, Benedick, the married man?" Beatrice remarks that she does not like beards (Act II, Scene I) and in Act III, Scene 2, Claudio and Don Pedro note that Benedick has shaved his beard off:

> **Don Pedro:** Hath any man seen him at the barber's?
>
> **Claudio:** No, but the barber's man hath been seen with him, and the old ornament of his cheek hath already stuffed tennis balls.

Apparently, Benedick has learned of Beatrice's dislike for beards and removed his in order to please her. There is much more of the same throughout the play. Though we cannot state that the language is "realistic," we observe that the social conduct of the characters is real, warm, and human. Their charm as human beings makes them lovable.

In a deeper vein, however, Shakespeare also infuses the play with his own subtle, prophetic insight. He does this in three ways. First, he sets up the behavior patterns of the romantic, courtly school of lovemaking, and then he proceeds to make it appear ludicrous. Second, he fills the serious scenes with melodrama to show the lengths to which tragicomedy will go. And last, through Beatrice and Benedick, he anticipates a new approach to the delineation of the love relationship. Shakespeare seemed to sense the end of a traditional way of life. Within twenty years after the writing of *Much Ado*, religious fanatics, Puritans, and disgruntled clergymen were hysterically shouting about the affectation, excesses, lewdness and immorality of the aristocracy (the theater was also included, and there was some truth in the sermonizing). By the early 1640's, the monarchy had been overthrown and all the theaters were closed. Though the monarchy returned in 1660, the old tradition of a courtly, romantic society, which had existed for centuries, was gone.

The scene of Claudio's denunciation of Hero at the altar and Leonato's distress over his daughter's supposed lack of virtue, though conceived in a vein of satire, is highly melodramatic. The same might be said of the encounter between Leonato and Antonio, and Don Pedro and Claudio. The punishment assigned to Claudio by Leonato, as well as Claudio's own notion of a ritual of mourning for Hero and the final revelation, are indeed contrivances that fit within the framework of tragicomedy. Again Shakespeare anticipated the future popularity of tragicomedy, which was to begin its rule of the stage within the next ten years (Beaumont and Fletcher are famous playwrights of this school).

Finally, the world within the play shows the lovers, Beatrice and Benedick, who have cast off the restraints of the romantic tradition that dictated the conduct of so many lovers in previous forms of literature. Their conversation is not pretentious. Their swift dialogue signifies a newly emerging outlook on life. Their wit displays a sharp awareness of their own situation. Though they both believe they are invincible, much to the enjoyment of the audience, their final submission shows their regard for the value of true love. We have reason to believe that Shakespeare's audience found this feature of *Much Ado About Nothing* the most enjoyable. In fact, for many years the play was often referred to as "Beatrice and Benedick."

Significance of the Title

The title of the play points to the fact that many difficulties arise from little or nothing — a word, a gesture, a preconception.

It is also suggestive of a pun on "nothing" (pronounced "noting" by Elizabethans). "Noting" could pertain to the theme of music in the play — notes of music, that is. To the Elizabethans, music was an appropriate synonym for a happy union: a marriage or the harmony reached at the end of a comedy. Thus the harmony that the lovers achieve is appropriately suggested in terms of music.

"Noting" could also refer to the way in which people "note" or "notice" things. For instance, Benedick notes what is said of him; Beatrice, what is said to her. Claudio notes that a lady at Hero's window is courting with a stranger, and he draws conclusions from this. The watch, in hiding, "notes" Borachio and Conrade, and they apprehend the villains. Each plot is marked by important "notings." The title thus refers to a most significant feature of the play.

Plot Summary

Don Pedro, Prince of Arragon, arrives in Messina, accompanied by his illegitimate brother, Don John, and his two friends, Claudio and Benedick, young Italian noblemen. Don Pedro has recently defeated his brother in battle. Reconciled, the brothers planned to visit Leonato before returning to their homeland. On their arrival in Messina, young Claudio is immediately attracted to the lovely Hero, daughter of Leonato. In order to help his faithful young friend in his suit, Don Pedro disguises himself as Claudio at a masked ball and woos Hero in Claudio's name. Thus he gains Leonato's consent for Claudio and Hero to marry. The bastard brother, Don John, tries to cause trouble by persuading Claudio that Don Pedro meant to betray him and keep Hero for himself, but the villain is foiled in his plot, and Claudio remains faithful to Don Pedro.

Benedick, the other young follower of Don Pedro, is a confirmed and bitter bachelor who scorns all men willing to enter the married state. Also opposed to matrimony is Leonato's niece, Beatrice. These two are at each other constantly, each one trying to gain supremacy by insulting the other. Don Pedro, with the help of Hero, Claudio, and Leonato, undertakes the seemingly impossible task of bringing Benedick and Beatrice together in matrimony in the seven days remaining before the marriage of Hero and Claudio.

Don John, unsuccessful in his first attempt to cause disharmony, now forms another plot. With the help of a serving-man, he arranges to make it appear that Hero is unfaithful to Claudio. The serving-man is to gain entrance to Hero's chambers when she is away. In her place will be her attendant, wearing Hero's clothes. Don John, posing as Claudio's true friend, will inform him of her unfaithfulness and lead him to Hero's window to witness her disloyalty.

In the meantime, Don Pedro carries out his plan to get Benedick and Beatrice to stop quarrelling and fall in love with each other. When Benedick is close by, thinking himself unseen, Don Pedro, Claudio, and Leonato will talk of their great sympathy for Beatrice, who loves Benedick but is unloved by him. The three tell one another sorrowful tales of the love letters Beatrice wrote to Benedick and then tore up. Sadly they remark that Beatrice beats her breast and sobs over her unrequited love for Benedick. Meanwhile, Hero and her serving-woman will, when Beatrice is nearby but thinking herself unseen, tell tales of poor Benedick, who pines and sighs for the heartless Beatrice. Thus both the unsuspecting young people will decide not to let the other suffer. Each will sacrifice principles and accept the other's love.

In the meantime, Don John is successful in his plot to ruin Hero. He tells Claudio that he has learned of Hero's unfaithfulness and he arranges to take him and Don Pedro to her window that very night, when they may witness her actions. Dogberry, a constable, and the members of the watch apprehend Don John's followers and overhear the truth of the plot. But in their stupidity, the petty officials can not get their story told in time to prevent Hero's disgrace. Although Don Pedro and Claudio do indeed witness the false betrayal, Claudio decides to let Hero go to the church on the next day, still thinking herself beloved. There, instead of marrying her, he will shame her before all the wedding guests.

All happens as Don John hoped. In front of the friar and all the guests, Claudio calls Hero unchaste and renounces her love for all time. The poor girl protests her innocence, but to no avail. Claudio protests that he saw with his own eyes her foul act. Then Hero faints, and appears to be dead. Claudio and Don Pedro leave her thus with Leonato, who also believes the story and wishes his daughter really dead in her shame. But the friar, believing the girl guiltless, convinces Leonato to believe in her too. He advises Leonato to let the world believe Hero dead, while they work to prove that she is innocent. Benedick, also believing her innocence, promises to help unravel the mystery. Then Beatrice tells Benedick of her love for him and asks him to kill Claudio, and so prove his love for her. Benedick challenges Claudio to a duel. Don John has fled the country after the successful outcome of his plot, but Benedick swears that he will find Don John and kill him, as well as Claudio.

At last Dogberry and the watch get to Leonato and tell their story. Claudio and Don Pedro hear it also, and Claudio wishes to die and to be with his wronged Hero. Leonato allows the two sorrowful men to continue to think Hero dead. In fact, they all attend her funeral. Leonato says that he will be avenged if Claudio will marry his niece, a girl who much resembles Hero. Although Claudio still loves the dead Hero, he agrees to marry the other girl in order to let Leonato have the favor he has so much right to ask.

When Don Pedro and Claudio arrive at Leonato's house for the ceremony, Leonato has all the ladies masked. He brings forth one of them, and tells Claudio that she is to be his wife. After Claudio promises to be her husband, the girl unmasks. She is, of course, Hero. At first, Claudio cannot believe his senses but, after he is convinced of the truth, he takes her to the church immediately. Then Benedick and Beatrice finally declare their true love for each other. They too go to the church after a dance in celebration of the double marriage to be performed. Best of all, word arrives that Don John has been captured and is being brought back to Messina to face his brother, Don Pedro. But his punishment must wait until tomorrow. Tonight all will be joy and happiness.

Summaries and Commentaries by Act and Scene

ACT I · SCENE 1

Summary

The setting of the play is Messina, Italy. The action begins in front of the house of Leonato, Governor of Messina. Leonato enters, accompanied by his daughter Hero, his niece Beatrice, and a messenger who has just delivered a letter containing the news that Don Pedro of Arragon will arrive that night in Messina. Don Pedro has just been victorious in battle, and very few "gentlemen" have been lost. Don Pedro has also included in his letter some remarks about "a young Florentine called Claudio" who, the messenger says, performed "the feats of a lion" in combat, despite his youth. The messenger remarks that Claudio's uncle, who lives in Messina, wept tears of joy when he was told of Claudio's bravery and reputation.

Beatrice asks the messenger if a certain "Signior Mountanto" has returned from the war. The messenger does not know to whom she is referring, and Hero states: "My cousin means Signior Benedick of Padua." Once Beatrice learns that Benedick has returned safely, she begins to make joking remarks about him: he came to Messina and advertised himself as a lady-killer and great lover; he boasts of his gallantry in battle; and he has a huge appetite. Leonato steps in to inform the messenger that Beatrice and Benedick are carrying on "a kind of merry war," and whenever they meet there is "a skirmish of wit/between them." Beatrice remarks that, in their last encounter, Benedick lost four of his five wits in the "merry war." She asks the messenger if Benedick has acquired a "new sworn brother," since every month he takes on a new blood-brother. The messenger jokingly replies that Benedick must certainly be out of Beatrice's favor. However, he is always seen in the company of Claudio. Beatrice remarks that if Claudio has "caught the Benedict" (a pun on the name of a disease), he will spend at least a thousand pounds before he is cured.

Don Pedro enters with Claudio, Benedick, Balthasar (Don Pedro's attendant) and "John the Bastard" (the illegitimate brother of Don Pedro). After an exchange of greetings between Leonato and Don Pedro, Benedick jestingly hints that Leonato was not sure that Hero was his daughter. Leonato answers that when his daughter Hero was born he knew she was his since Benedick was then only a child (teasing Benedick about his supposed notoriety with women). Benedick tries to come back with another jest. Beatrice, however breaks into the conversation and addresses herself directly to Benedick: "I wonder that you will still be talking, Signior Benedick. Nobody marks you." Benedick immediately comes back at Beatrice with the reply: "What my dear Lady Disdain! are you yet living?" Beatrice answers by stating that her disdain cannot die as long as she can practise it upon Benedick. Benedick jestingly responds to her remark about her disdain by saying that he is loved by all ladies except Beatrice, but that this is inconsequential to him, for he loves none of them. Beatrice says that his lack of affection is a blessing for women. She, too, cannot stand men and would "rather hear my dog bark at a cow than a man swear he loves me."

Benedick quickly states that he hopes God will keep Beatrice in that frame of mind in order to save some man a scratched face. (He is calling her a shrew in a gentlemanly fashion.) Beatrice does not like this remark, and replies that scratching would improve a man's face if the face were Benedick's. They exchange a few more parting remarks and then break off.

Don Pedro informs Claudio and Benedick that, at Leonato's invitation, they will remain his guests for at least a month. Leonato thanks Don Pedro for consenting to remain that long, and then addresses himself to Don John: "Let me bid you welcome, my lord. Being reconciled to the Prince, your brother, I owe you all duty." Don John dutifully thanks Leonato and moves away.

Leonato and Don Pedro go off arm in arm, followed by everyone except Claudio and Benedick. Claudio asks Benedick's opinion of Hero, Leonato's daughter. Benedick, of course, teases Claudio: "Why, i' faith, methinks she's too low for a high praise, too brown for a fair praise, and too little for a great praise." Claudio professes love for Hero: "In mine eyes she is the sweetest lady that ever I looked on." Benedick remarks that he hopes his friend has not fallen in love. Benedick good-naturedly berates Claudio for rushing towards becoming a cuckold (the husband of an unfaithful wife). Don Pedro returns and inquires why his two friends have not entered Don Leonato's house. Benedick asks Don Pedro to command him to tell the reason, whereupon Don Pedro orders Benedick to reveal the secret discussion.

When Don Pedro learns of Claudio's love for Hero, he says: "Amen, if you love her, for the lady is very well worthy." Then follows an exchange among the friends to the effect that Benedick, though grateful to a woman for conceiving him, will never give up his freedom for a cuckold's horns. Don Pedro teases Benedick that one day he will fall madly in love. He then asks Benedick to inform Leonato he will soon come in to supper.

After Benedick leaves, Claudio, learning that Hero is Leonato's only heir, requests Don Pedro to ask in his behalf for Hero's hand in marriage. Don Pedro informs Claudio that he will do even more than that. There will be celebrations and dancing that night. During the masked ball, Don Pedro will disguise himself as Claudio and confess his love to Hero. He will then tell Leonato of Claudio's love, and Hero thus will be given to Claudio.

Commentary

The first scene prepares the audience favorably for the role of Claudio as lover, for he has already proved himself in war. There are mixed feelings about him, however, due to the statement that he has done "in the figure of a lamb the feats of a lion." May not Claudio be a deceiver? As a conventional lover, Claudio will work through a proxy (Don Pedro) in his suit to Hero, a situation which invites complications and arouses suspense as to the outcome of his courtship.

The audience is also prepared for the role of Benedick (likewise a successful soldier) as a mocker who engages in "merry war" with Beatrice, and as a changeable character whose stated antagonism towards women may quickly yield to love. The suspicion that ultimately Benedick and Beatrice will become lovers is planted in the mind of the audience (a) through the wit-combat, which by its intensity suggests the presence of strong feelings beneath the surface, and (b) through Don Pedro's playful threat that he will see Benedick "look pale with love." This couple's reactions provide the second of two distinct sets of responses to love: the ardent but subdued (Claudio and Hero), and the antagonistic and talkative (Benedick and Beatrice).

The society of Messina is introduced as one of cultured cordiality and hospitality. Leonato's welcoming of Don Pedro and his followers is courteous to a fault, and might possibly be explained by the presence of two unmarried and eligible ladies in his family.

A young Paduan soldier of fortune, Benedick is aggressively witty. He has been one of Don Pedro's courtiers, but is not as close to the Prince as Claudio is. He and Claudio have been dear friends. Returning from war, Benedick exercises his wit in the form of satire, especially at the expense of Beatrice, to whom he is genuinely attracted. One might suspect that, since his feelings are hurt in the exchange of wit with Beatrice, Benedick has been in the habit of covering up a sensitive nature by the use of clever remarks.

The lovely Beatrice is attracted to Benedick, but conceals her feelings under a barrage of wit. She is carefree, proud and disdainful. Others may point out the benefits of marriage to her, but she retains her composure and her clear-eyed indifference to it. Being of a cordial nature, she is gracious to her uncle's guests, and she is obedient to Leonato. Beatrice is the most sparkling character in the play.

A successful military leader, Don Pedro is genuinely grateful for the hospitable reception of Leonato. Witty enough, he is more practical-minded than his subordinates, and he does not have to be told twice that Claudio requires his aid in the winning of Hero. Though generous and forgiving (he has accepted his bastard brother, Don

John, who has been at outs with him, back into his good graces), Don Pedro is somewhat too attentive to Claudio. His scheme to woo Hero for Claudio smacks of overprotectiveness. Since Claudio has no father, however, this may have been the proper procedure of the time.

Leonato's daughter is a quiet, but agreeable, young woman of marriageable age and pleasing appearance. Her relative silence in this scene is a cue to the pattern of her behavior throughout: she will be the watchful, and not the talkative type.

Most of the first scene is in the dramatic prose style that Shakespeare had developed by 1598. Beatrice, as the most skilful manipulator of words in the play, best illustrates the quality of the prose.

The rest of the scene is in blank verse (unrhymed iambic pentameter). Blank verse is used in the dialogue between Claudio and Don Pedro to convey the intensity of Claudio's feelings toward Hero. The following passage reveals its level:

> But now I am return'd and that war-thoughts
> Have left their places vacant, in their rooms
> Come thronging soft and delicate desires,...

Shakespeare is notorious for his use of puns. The audience should be on the alert for this type of word play. Three examples in this scene are: "but he'll be meet with you;" (*meet* meaning "proper," "meat," and "encounter"); "He is a very valiant trencherman" (*trencherman* meaning "soldier," "diner," and (possibly) "sexual partner"); and "He is no less than a stuffed man" (*stuffed* meaning "full of food," "bombastic," and "filled with artificial material in order to appear significant or adequate").

Another feature to notice is the presence of apothegms (wise sayings) and proverbs. "There are no faces truer than those that are so washed," says Leonato. "What need the bridge much broader than the flood," says Don Pedro. In almost every scene Shakespeare wrote there are traditional sayings, or "wise saws," that support the line of argument.

Imagery is also used to establish atmosphere and tone. In highly figurative language like Shakespeare's, it is difficult to distinguish the image from a colorful use of speech. In general, Shakespeare uses images in this scene to establish the aristocratic atmosphere of Messina. The concerns of high society are reflected in a series of images exploring the whole range of decorum, dress and fashion, food, learning, military preoccupations, money, music, and sports. Images from the animal world and nature provide a contrast to the cultured society of Messina. Images of sickness and crime reveal the darker side of this aristocratic life.

Religious imagery suggests the uniqueness of such a character as

Benedick, who will "die at the stake" in defiance of love. Animal imagery again separates Benedick from the conventional society through his identification with the "savage bull" eventually forced into harness (i.e., civilized).

ACT I · SCENE 2

Summary

This scene takes place in Leonato's house. Leonato enters with his brother, Antonio. They are discussing arrangements for the festivities. Antonio has some strange news for Leonato. Antonio's servant has overheard Don Pedro profess to Claudio his love for Leonato's daughter Hero. This night at the dance he will reveal his love to Hero and inform Leonato immediately. Leonato does not quite know what to say about this unexpected, though not completely unwelcome, news. He decides to wait until Don Pedro reveals himself, but meanwhile he thinks it best to inform Hero of Don Pedro's intentions so that she will have a ready answer. They leave, and attendants enter to prepare for the night's festivities.

Commentary

This scene introduces Antonio, Leonato's brother, who is later to challenge Claudio. The news reported by Antonio, to the mistaken effect that Don Pedro intends to woo Hero for himself, introduces a possible threat to the success of Claudio's intentions, as well as suspense as to whether Don Pedro really intends to help win Hero as promised. The scene also indicates that Hero is to be prepared for Don Pedro's proposal. Leonato's preparations for the evening's entertainment serve to fill in time before the reception.

Leonato reveals himself as the fussy host now seeing to all the details of the entertainment of his guests. Surprised to hear that Don Pedro intends to court Hero, he is nevertheless reluctant to interrogate the servant who overheard the Prince's conversation. The question arises as to whether he is excessively ambitious for his daughter.

Leonato's brother is an old man who seems to have a suspicious nature; he is certainly a bearer of gossip.

"Dream" imagery is significant here. It suggests that strange things are going on, and that more is involved than meets the eye. News that Don Pedro is to court Hero leads Leonato to respond, "We will hold it as a dream till it appear itself." Thus the theme of appearance and reality, introduced in the first scene in reference, for instance, to Claudio's behavior in war ("doing in the figure of a lamb the feats of a lion"), continues here.

ACT I · SCENE 3

Summary

Don John and his servant, Conrade, enter a room in Leonato's house. Conrade is trying to cheer up his master, but Don John wishes to remain sullen. He says that he will be "sad when I have cause, and smile at no man's jests; eat when I have stomach, and wait for no man's leisure; sleep when I am drowsy, and tend on no man's business; laugh when I am merry, and claw no man in his humor." (The last statement refers to flattering no man.) Conrade tactfully states that Don John has recently "stood out" against his brother, Don Pedro, and now that he is back in his good graces should try to seek some kind of advancement. Don John replies that he would rather be as he is, a scorned, miserable individual, than a contented personality in the sight of Don Pedro. Don John cannot put on a "carriage" to acquire the good graces of anyone. Besides, he says, it fits his "blood to be disdained of all." (He is referring to the scorn his illegitimacy has brought upon him.) He calls himself "a plain-dealing villain."

Borachio, another of Don John's followers, enters. (Note: Borachio is taken from the Spanish word "borracho," which means "drunk.") He informs Don John that while he was airing out a room, he overheard Don Pedro and Claudio talking of Don Pedro's intent to woo Hero in Claudio's place and obtain her for the young count. Don John immediately jumps at the chance of causing some trouble for Claudio, whom he sarcastically calls "a proper squire," "A very forward March-chick," and a "young start-up" who has acquired a great amount of glory and recognition for his part in overthrowing Don John in battle. Don John's followers swear to aid him "to the death," and they all go off to create some mischief.

Commentary

In providing Don John with news that Claudio hopes to win Hero through Don Pedro's wooing, this scene lays the groundwork for Don John's plot against Claudio. The reason behind Don John's schemes is supplied by the information about his previous overthrow in his rebellion against Don Pedro. The envy he feels toward Claudio as the preferred follower of Don Pedro supplies an additional motive for his villainy. Suspense develops over the issue of what means Don John may exploit in order to ruin Claudio's plans. This scene also suggests that various people know of different versions of Don Pedro's scheme to win Hero for Claudio.

Revealed to be melancholy by nature, Don John is discontented over his recent defeat at the hands of the Prince, his brother. Though now taken back into his brother's good graces, Don John resents the fact that Claudio has, in effect, replaced him in the affections of Don Pedro. Because of his disposition and his frustration (as well as, it might be added, the stigma of his illegitimate birth), he seeks an opportunity for revenge. His discontent has drawn a certain class of followers (such as Conrade and Borachio), who are ready to aid him in his plottings.

Evidently someone of gentle birth driven to perform menial tasks, Borachio conveys the news about Claudio's plans for winning Hero. In Borachio, Don John has a loyal, indeed slavish, follower in the pursuit of evil goals.

Another companion of Don John's is Conrade, a subservient individual who advises Don John to await the opportunity to gain revenge on Don Pedro. When he sees that Don John is not swayed by reason, he falls in with the other's mood and suggests action of some sort. Later in the scene, he confirms his loyalty by offering to assist Don John "to the death."

Prose, used throughout this scene, is marked by the mannered balance and contrast in Don John's speeches. Such passages as "I had rather be a canker in a hedge than a rose in his grace" suggest the calculated and controlled passion of a villainous individual.

The pun on "cheer" — "Their *cheer* is the greater that I am subdued" — involves three possible meanings of the word; it would signify "complexion," "food," or "delight." The term "subdued" refers both to the fact that Don John has been defeated in war and that he has been downcast in mood.

Animal imagery suggests that Don John, like Benedick, tends to be an outsider in the aristocratic world of Messina: "I am trusted with a *muzzle* and enfranchised with a *clog*; therefore I have decreed not *to sing in my cage*. If I had my *mouth*, I would *bite*." The "muzzle" suggests a dog; the "clog," a beast of burden; and the "cage," a captive bird. Don John therefore tends to be identified with the world of nature. Thus he, the natural man (a bastard was called a "natural son"), rejects the extension of heavenly forgiveness, or "grace," on the part of his legitimate brother, Don Pedro — a religious image. As an artist or schemer, Don John is searching for a "model to build mischief on." Thus the imagery of this scene locates Don John in the appropriate intellectual and spiritual sphere: he is a bastard, a child of nature, an outsider, and a schemer.

ACT II · SCENE 1

Summary

This long scene takes place in the hall in Leonato's house, which has been decorated for the masked ball. Leonato, Antonio, Beatrice, Hero and Hero's personal servants, Margaret and Ursula, enter a little before the dancing begins. Leonato inquires if Don John was present at supper. Beatrice remarks that Don John's sour facial expressions leave her "heartburned an hour after." Hero demurely adds a remark that Don John is rather ill-tempered. Beatrice remarks that the perfect man would be the one who combined some of Don John's silence and a portion of Benedick's chattering. Then if he had a good leg for dancing and money in his purse, "such a man would win any woman in the world — if'a could get her good will." Leonato scolds Beatrice by saying that she is too shrewish, to which Beatrice replies that God will not send her a husband because she is so "curst" ("God sends a curst cow short horns").

Beatrice has now begun to exercise her wit, and remarks that she thanks God every morning and evening for not sending her a husband. Anyway, she could never endure a husband with a beard. "You may light on a husband that hath no beard," is Leonato's reply. Beatrice cleverly responds by saying that a man without a beard is "less than a man," and he who has a beard, is "more than a youth." To her way of thinking, whoever is "more than a youth" is not for her, and she is not for anyone who is "less than a man." As punishment for dying unwed, Beatrice says she will lead apes into hell. However, her trip to hell must stop at the gate when the devil, with horns on his head like a cuckold, sends her to heaven because there is no room in hell for maids. Once she is in heaven, St. Peter will show her where the unmarried (of both sexes) stay, and together they will all be merry "as the day is long." Antonio tells Hero he hopes she will be less shrewish than her cousin, and that she will be "ruled" by her father. Beatrice remarks that it is Hero's duty to do everything Leonato commands, even marry the man he chooses. But Beatrice also tells Hero to be sure that the husband Leonato finds for her is at least handsome.

To Leonato's reply that he hopes to see his niece married one day, Beatrice answers that men are only dust, and a woman would be "grieved" to be ruled by "a clod of wayward marl" (earth). Besides, all the sons of Adam are her brothers, and she "holds it a sin to match in my kindred." Leonato reminds Hero of her answer if the Prince should offer marriage. Beatrice very cleverly remarks that "wooing, wedding, and repenting is as a Scotch jig, a measure, and a cinque-pace." The suit for marriage is as "hot and hasty" as the Scotch jig; the wedding is stately, full of broad measure; and "repentance" is like an old man dancing the cinque-pace faster and faster until he dies. (In other words, a mistake in marriage can be fatal.) Leonato remarks that Beatrice is very clever, and Beatrice replies: "I have a good eye, uncle; I can see a church by daylight."

The revellers approach, and those on stage put on their masks. Don Pedro, Claudio, Benedick and Balthasar enter wearing their masks. Don John and Borachio accompany them, but they are unmasked. Music strikes up and the company pairs off: Hero and Don Pedro; Balthasar and Margaret; Ursula and Antonio; and Beatrice and Benedick. Beatrice, dancing with the masked Benedick and unaware of his identity, is trying to find out from him who has said that she is not only "disdainful," but also that she steals her "good wit out of the

'Hundred Merry Tales.' " She decides that only Benedick would say such a thing about her. Benedick pretends not to know whom she means, but Beatrice replies, "I am sure you know him well enough." She then says that Benedick is the "Prince's jester, a very dull fool." His greatest gift is to think up "slanders," which only "libertines" like him delight in, and he is more villainous than witty. Benedick says that when he meets the gentleman, he will tell him.

They leave the stage with those leading the dance. Claudio is left on stage to wonder about the Prince's talk with Hero and Leonato. Borachio and Don John also remain on stage. Don John remarks loudly, for Claudio to hear, that he thinks Don Pedro is in love with Hero and has taken Leonato aside to ask for her hand in marriage.

Don John, pretending that he is talking to Benedick (Claudio is wearing a mask), asks Claudio to convince Don Pedro not to marry Hero, who is below him in birth. Claudio asks Don John how he knows that Don Pedro loves Hero. Don John replies that his brother told him so. Borachio says that he also heard Don Pedro swear he would marry Hero tonight. The two liars then go off to partake of the banquet, leaving Claudio heartbroken. "Friendship is constant in all other things/Save in the office and affairs of love," he says. Everyone should "negotiate" for himself, because beauty has the power to charm the best intentions of a friend into passionate love. He bids Hero farewell.

Benedick enters and teases Claudio about how sad he looks. He jokes that the Prince "hath got your Hero," and Claudio replies, "I wish him joy of her." Benedick scolds Claudio because his reply sounds like that of a cattle dealer selling "bullocks." He then asks if Claudio really thinks that the Prince is deceiving him. Claudio is hurt by the remark and asks Benedick to leave him. But Benedick chastises Claudio for his jealousy. He says that Claudio is acting like a blind man striking out in all directions because his dinner has been stolen. Claudio leaves in anger.

Now Benedick admits how Beatrice hurt him. He is upset because she said he was the Prince's jester. He wonders if there may not appear to be some truth in the remarks, since he indeed has a merry soul. Finally, he decides it is Beatrice's shrewishness that makes her think her opinion of him is shared by everyone. Don Pedro, Hero and Leonato enter, and the Prince asks for Claudio. Benedick tells the Prince that Claudio thinks he has stolen Hero. Don Pedro says Claudio is mistaken and he will soon put things right. Then, in a jovial mood, Don Pedro tells Benedick that Beatrice is furious over what her dancing partner told her Benedick had said about her. Benedick reveals that he was the dancing partner and Beatrice "misused him past the endurance of a block!" He repeats the things Beatrice said about him and

29

also swears he would not marry her if she had all the good features of Adam before the Fall.

Beatrice enters with Claudio, and Benedick, seeing her approach, asks if Don Pedro would send him on an errand to Asia or to the land of the "Pygmies" so that he might escape "my Lady Tongue." Benedick leaves quickly, whereupon Don Pedro teases Beatrice for having lost Benedick's heart. Beatrice replies to the effect that Benedick had only lent it to her, so she has paid him back with interest. She hints that he had been false to her before, and now she is getting even. The Prince and Beatrice both joke about Claudio's jealousy. Don Pedro informs Claudio that he has wooed for him and Leonato has given his consent. Claudio can barely speak, but finally he says: "Silence is the perfectest herald of joy."

The two lovers move to the side and whisper to each other as Beatrice and Don Pedro engage in jests. Beatrice sighs that everyone is getting married but her. Don Pedro remarks that he will get her a husband, and Beatrice answers she would like a husband like Don Pedro. When he asks her: "Will you have me, lady?" she replies: "No, my lord, unless I might have another for working days; your Grace is too costly to wear every day." Leonato sends Beatrice on an errand and asks Claudio when he wishes to be married. Claudio responds: "To-morrow, my lord. Time goes on crutches till Love have all his rites." But Leonato replies that they must wait at least one week so he may arrange all the necessary formalities. Don Pedro then hits upon a scheme whereby the week will pass quickly and in good sport. He will tell them all how they can trick Beatrice and Benedick into falling in love with each other. Leonato, Claudio and Hero agree to the plan.

Commentary

This scene shows the successful completion of Don Pedro's plan to woo Hero for Claudio, and again, Leonato's consent to the marriage. Due to the complicated plan that Don Pedro has devised, there are opportunities for much deception to arise, emphasizing the theme of appearance and reality. The deceptions enable Claudio to suffer a dramatic reversal and become the soul of melancholy. His first reversal is balanced by a later one, as a result of which Claudio's spirits are restored and he becomes betrothed to Hero. Thus the fluctuating character of Claudio is well-documented.

The scene also shows Don John as he impresses others (as a melancholy, silent man, the reverse in many ways of Benedick, to whom Beatrice compares him). It also shows him in action as a trickster. Although Don John has not hit upon the right scheme yet to ruin Claudio, there is little doubt that he will soon discover some means of disturbing the young soldier's happiness. Thus this scene, in which Don John spreads false impressions, prepares for his further knavery later.

A third plot is in the making at the end of this scene. It had already been hinted at when Don Pedro warned Benedick that he would turn lover one day, but it is at this point that the plot finally crystallizes. Benedick and Beatrice are to be tricked into falling in love with each other. In view of the fact that seven days must elapse before Claudio marries Hero, the intrigue surrounding Beatrice and Benedick will serve the extra purpose of filling in the interval of time.

Three developments create suspense: Will the wedding take place as scheduled? Will Don John evolve a plot to destroy the happiness of Claudio? Will Don Pedro and his fellow conspirators manage to deceive Benedick and Beatrice into admitting mutual love?

The reactions of Beatrice to the prospect of Hero's being wooed by Don Pedro, and to the return of Benedick to Messina, are almost hysterical. The hilarity of her dialogue in the first part of the scene, and the cruelty of her remarks to Benedick, suggest that she is disturbed by the new pressures upon her. She distinguishes herself from her cousin Hero on the score of her independence: whether her father chose a mate for her or not, she would select her *own* husband.

Hurt by Beatrice's comment that he is the Prince's fool, Benedick pretends to himself that she did not recognize him in his mask. His injured sensitivity makes him (like Don John) misinterpret Don Pedro's wooing of Hero, and he takes out his anguish on Claudio, whom he victimizes with mock-sympathy at Don Pedro's sneaky theft of Hero. Benedick's antagonism to Beatrice reaches heroic (even Herculean) proportions.

At the masque, Claudio is subject to severe stress. His instability is suggested by the readiness with which he pretends (because of Don John's apparent mistake) to be Benedick — evidently in order to learn something he might not otherwise have learned. When he hears that Don Pedro has courted Hero for himself, Claudio at once believes the report, a sign of insecurity and a preparation for his later hasty belief in Hero's infidelity. Benedick's similar report merely confirms the despair that Don John has aroused. But with the assurances Don Pedro gives, Claudio returns to high spirits. Claudio's swings of emotion from melancholy to joyous hope are among the significant revelations of this scene. His passivity to the Prince is balanced by the egotism of his address to Hero upon being told she is his: "I give myself away for you...." Thus Claudio displays instability, passivity, unusual haste in believing the worst, and self-centeredness.

Very much the proper, obedient daughter in taking her father's instructions, Hero is almost Claudio's alter ego in being mute and passive. For example, when Claudio professes his affection for her, she can do little but whisper a few well-chosen, but unheard, words of love into his ear. She later agrees to do "any modest office" in Don Pedro's plot to bring together Benedick and Beatrice.

The role of Leonato is that of the shrewd father. If Don Pedro indeed plans to ask for Hero's hand, he will find Hero prepared. Leonato is willing to accept Claudio as a son-in-law, but he wishes a proper (or at least a token) interval to elapse before the ceremony. Leonato also agrees to participate in the trick on Benedick and Beatrice. He is thus also the considerate uncle and the responsible host.

Except for one melancholy soliloquy by Claudio, the entire scene is in prose. A technical device that deserves notice is the poet's use of stichomythia (dialogue delivered in alternating lines, or verbal fencing) during the masque and elsewhere. Puns are frequent throughout this scene.

The imagery of this scene is highly revealing. Schematically, it runs through such general categories as animals, decorum, discourse, dress and fashion, food, heraldry, inanimate objects, magic and myth, military matters, money, music, religion, sickness, sports, and weather.

A more meaningful arrangement of images would perhaps be in terms of the characters who use the images. As the most active speakers in the play, Benedick and Beatrice introduce most of the images. Benedick reveals himself as playing four main roles: as an outsider, he is a critic of society; as a potential lover, he reacts to the personality of Beatrice; as a soldier, he conceives of things in feelings and terms appropriate to that calling; and as a messenger, he plays the role of an unwitting deceiver.

As critic, Benedick points out to Claudio that the young lover should now wear a garland of willow like a usurer's chain or a lieutenant's scarf, to carry out his new part as the melancholy, rejected lover. As a potential lover of Beatrice, Benedick has his feelings hurt. He therefore describes her in unfavorable terms. It is noticeable that both he and Beatrice often think in terms that suggest the physical, militant side of things. To him, Beatrice is my "Lady Tongue." If her breath were as "infectious" as her words, who could live near her? She is an ogress, and even the Garden of Eden would not make life worth living with such a shrew as she. Benedick would do any of the labors of Hercules to stay clear of her. As a soldier, he describes Beatrice's statements as "poniards," and he says he recently felt like a man being shot at by an army instead of by a mere woman of words. Benedick serves as a messenger bringing to Claudio the false report of Don Pedro's theft of Hero: "I have played the part of Lady Fame," he assures Don Pedro.

Beatrice, the most ingenious image-maker in the play, also serves as a critic. She rejects Don Pedro as a potential husband because he is "too costly to wear every day." From an image of clothing she turns to the physiological in her reaction to Don John, whose sourness leaves her "heart-burned an hour after." She prefers the mean between extremes: Don John is too like an image; Benedick is "too like my lady's eldest son, evermore tattling." Her most notable set piece in this scene is the passage in which she compares wooing, wedding, and repenting to three kinds of dance. Finally, observing Claudio's jealousy, she compares his appearance to that of an orange.

As a potential lover, Beatrice sees men as clods of earth, pieces of "valiant dust." The religious imagery emerges more clearly in her mention of Adam. To her, men are wicked and unredeemed. They need grace and purification (a significant theme in the play). Beatrice's reaction to men as "valiant dust" indicates that she has her eye on Benedick, the warrior: "I am sure he is in the fleet. I would he had boarded me;" and "He'll but break a comparison or two [like a lance] on me; which peradventure, not marked or not laughed at, strikes him into melancholy;" and "then there's a partridge wing saved, for the fool will eat no supper that night." In this passage, military, discourse, sickness and food images illuminate the roles of Benedick and the attitude of Beatrice toward him.

ACT II · SCENE 2

Summary

Don John and Borachio enter a room in Leonato's house. Don John says that Claudio's marriage to Hero is arranged. Borachio answers that he can "cross it," and Don John maliciously replies that "Any bar, any cross, any impediment will be medicinable to me." Borachio says he can stop the marriage and appear innocent of any involvement. He tells Don John he is in much favor with Margaret, Hero's waiting gentlewoman. He will have Margaret come to Hero's window late at night — after he has contrived Hero's absence — and pretend that she is Hero and he is Claudio. Meanwhile, according to Borachio's instructions, Don John will go to Don Pedro and Claudio and accuse Hero of being a "contaminated stale" (a prostitute). The night before the wedding, Don John will bring Don Pedro and Claudio to a place where they can observe Hero's balcony window. There they will see Margaret and Borachio pretending to be Hero and her lover. Claudio and Don Pedro will, of course, think that the girl, seen at night and from a distance, is Hero. Naturally they will want to cancel the marriage when they observe a man enter Hero's bedchamber. Don John is very pleased with this scheme and he offers Borachio a thousand ducats if it is carried out successfully. Don John leaves with Borachio to find out the day of the marriage.

Commentary

The scene reaffirms Don John's melancholy, discontented nature and shows him at last finding the scheme he has been searching for in his effort to harm Claudio. Borachio comes to the fore as the brains of the Don John plot.

The scene also provides information as to a more complicated situation in Leonato's household than previously has been suspected: a relationship of some sort between Margaret and Borachio. This is evidence of disorder in the household, and disorder always spells trouble in Shakespeare's plays. The appearance and reality theme is reinforced by Borachio when he says that "there shall appear such seeming truth of Hero's disloyalty that jealousy shall be called assurance and all the preparation overthrown."

Wherever he appears, Don John creates a mood of suspicion and intrigue. Still obsessed with the desire for revenge, he remains sullen, and passive. It is only through the inventiveness of Borachio that a plot is evolved. Don John reveals himself as Machiavellian in his acceptance of such a plot, and materialistic in his promise of a large reward to Borachio for success in the scheme.

Revealing himself again as a devious, if loyal, follower of Don John, Borachio is willing to use his friendship with Margaret in order to further Don John's conspiracy. But he is materialistic enough to realize that a reward will be forthcoming. When he is promised a reward of a thousand ducats, he promises to carry out his end of the bargain.

The mannered prose speech associated with Don John marks this scene and again suggests the stilted, tension-ridden inner life of this villain. Borachio's prose is straightforward and to the point.

At least one pun may be noticed here. Speaking of the marriage, Borachio declares that he can "cross it." "Cross" suggests (a) a heraldry term, (b) a thwarting, (c) a crucifixion. Heraldry might be appropriate in view of Don John's intention to discredit the new honors Claudio has gained. The thwarting of the marriage plans would gratify the villain's desire for revenge, and the idea of crucifixion suggests a sacrifice such as Hero will be made to suffer.

Images of food, heraldry, and sickness appear in this scene. The plot suggested by Borachio is identified with poison. "The poison of that [information] lies in you to temper," says Borachio to Don John. The latter picks up the sickness motif: "I am sick in displeasure to him [Claudio]." Indeed, "any bar, any cross, any impediment will be medicinable to me," he declares. The bar and cross suggest heraldry; "medicinable" relates to the sickness he feels at his humiliating new situation. The "cross" also suggests that Don John is symbolically a sort of devil who is the antagonist to the kind and gracious Don Pedro. Don John represents a Judas who, in the guise of defending the honor of Claudio and the Prince, crucifies them through the damage done to Hero.

ACT II · SCENE 3

Summary

Benedick enters Leonato's garden, calls for a serving boy, and orders the lad to bring him a book that lies in his room. His mind wanders over the events of the past few days. He is amazed that Claudio, who had previously scorned the folly of falling in love, has now become the object of his own scorn: "I have known when there was no music with him but the drum and the fife; and now had he rather hear the tabor and the pipe." Instead of being interested in good armor, Claudio is now intent upon the fashion of his clothes. Previously, Claudio was a plain speaker, but now his thoughts have turned to the abstract. "May I be so converted and see with these eyes? I cannot tell; I think not," says Benedick when he momentarily ponders if he will ever fall in love. One thought leads to another, and Benedick humorously recounts the wonderful virtues his wife will have to possess if ever he marries: she will have to be rich, virtuous, beautiful, wise, articulate, mild, noble and musically inclined. Of course, he is making fun of the image of the idealized woman whom poets romanticized in love sonnets and ballads. This is revealed in his last remark, which casts a humorous denial upon the convention of the "ideal" woman: "...and her hair shall be of what color it please God." The Elizabethan age adored fair-skinned beauty and blonde hair. Note that Beatrice remarks that she is "sunburnt," (hence she thinks herself dark or ugly). Benedick is saying that if he can find all these other attributes in a woman, it will not really matter what color her hair is. Benedick sees the Prince and "Monsieur Love" entering, and he hides in the arbor. Don Pedro, Leonato, Claudio and Balthasar enter as music is played in the background. They wish to hear some of Balthasar's music, Claudio says, for the evening is still, "as hushed on purpose to grace harmony." Don Pedro remarks that Benedick is hidden, and Claudio replies that they should spring the trap after the music. Don Pedro then tries to convince Balthasar to sing, but Balthasar hesitates because he feels his voice is imperfect. Finally he is persuaded, and he sings a song that warns ladies to beware of those "deceivers," men. After the song, Balthasar is complimented for singing so well, but Benedick, scorning love songs, remarks in an "aside" that the Prince would have hanged a dog had he howled so badly. Don Pedro sends Balthasar off to make arrangements for "excellent music" to be sung at "Lady Hero's chamber window" tomorrow night.

After Balthasar leaves, Don Pedro begins the deception:

Come hither, Leonato. What was it you told me of today? that your niece Beatrice was in love with Signior Benedick?

35

Claudio urges them on and says, "I did never think that lady would have loved any man." To which Leonato replies:

> No, nor I neither; but most wonderful that she should so dote on Signior Benedick, whom she hath in all outward behaviors seemed ever to abhor.

Benedick is immediately interested: "Is't possible? Sits the wind in that corner?" From this point on, the three friends exaggerate how fiercely Beatrice loves Benedick and how undeserving Benedick is of her love. Beatrice loves Benedick with "an enraged affection" past the "infinite of thought." And she is not pretending either, for she actually shows the effects of passion. Benedick again speaks in an "aside" and wonders if all this talk is not a trick. But Leonato, "the white-bearded fellow," is also speaking, so it must be true. Claudio notes that Benedick has "ta'en th' infection" and that they should continue. Beatrice, they say, swears she will not let her love be known to Benedick. "Shall I...that have so oft encountered him with scorn, write to him that I love him?" are supposedly her remarks. According to Hero, Beatrice stays up all night writing letters to Benedick and tearing them up. Indeed, Hero thinks that Beatrice is so desperate she might even hurt herself. They decide not to tell Benedick because he would probably make fun of Beatrice's affection. She is a sweet, pretty and virtuous lady whose only fault is loving Benedick, they say; but she is also proud. She will not relent in her merry war with Benedick, even though she loves him. Then they grudgingly compliment Benedick for being handsome, wise, witty and valiant. As for Beatrice's love, perhaps she will be able to get over it. As they leave, Don Petro advises Leonato to have Hero and her gentlewomen prepare "the same net" for Beatrice. They decide to send Beatrice to call Benedick in for dinner.

Benedick comes out from hiding and remarks that the conversation cannot be a trick since they seemed so serious. "Love me," he says. "Why, it must be requited." He is upset because he was criticized for having a contemptuous nature. He decides the best course for a man to take is to mend his errors and overcome his pride, once he learns of these faults. He says he will be "horribly" in love with Beatrice, though he had thought he would never fall in love. Indeed, Beatrice is a very virtuous and pretty lady. He realizes suddenly that he will now be the object of jests because of his change in attitude. That does not matter, however, for "the world must be peopled."

Benedick spies Beatrice approaching and immediately notes "some marks of love in her." Beatrice enters and tells him dinner is ready. "Fair Beatrice, I thank you for your pains." Beatrice looks at him quizzically and responds that she would not have come if it had been painful. Benedick asks her if she has had pleasure in delivering the message. Beatrice answers that she takes as much pleasure in delivering the message as one takes in the point of a knife. Since Benedick does not wish to argue or come in to dinner with her, she leaves. Benedick immediately notes a double meaning in her remarks to him, proving that she loves him. He therefore decides to take pity upon her and return the love. He exits in search of her picture.

Commentary

The basic purpose for this scene is the consummation of one part of the Beatrice-Benedick plot. If the Prince's scheme is to succeed, the two scoffers must be made to fall in love with each other and then to confess their mutual affection. The tone used in the accomplishment of this is that of High Comedy. The mocker of love, longing to become a convert, is tricked by his friends into accepting hearsay as evidence that Beatrice loves him. The pleasurable sensation that results is due in large part to the knowledge that Benedick, who has been attracted to Beatrice, now can yield to his desire to admit it. The trickster tricked is an old formula for dramatic success.

Suspense develops as to how Beatrice will react to the prank the women are to play on her. Will she fall as decisively as did Benedick? The entire scene prepares for the future double wedding. Shakespeare often employs two sets of lovers in his comedies.

A modest figure, Balthasar is reluctant to sing unless urged. His courtesy illustrates the caution and sense of decorum expected of the courtier. His polite artificiality suggests one extreme; the almost artificial villainy of Don John represents the other.

Benedick is now more sensitive to the flattery and criticism of his friends than he had seemed to be earlier. Their comments prompt him to accept Beatrice's love at face value. No doubt his new determination to turn lover is due to the previous unstable relationship he has had with people. In addition, it is due to some insecurity, perhaps attributable to Claudio's sudden conversion to love and his recent preference of Don Pedro's company.

Carrying out his plot, Don Pedro shows the ability to lead others and to perform a delicate task with distinction. He also shows foresight in looking ahead to the next stage of the proceedings — namely, to the tempting of Beatrice.

Poetry is used only in the section that precedes and includes Balthasar's song. Except for the song, which is rhymed in ballad meter, the poetry is in blank verse. Note the beautiful effect of the lines "How still the evening is / As hushed on purpose to grade harmony!" Prose, used elsewhere in the scene, is highly expressive and lively.

The imagery in this scene is concerned primarily with Benedick, victim of a plot, who continues to be associated with the animal world and with the military.

Benedick, evaluating the possibility that he may turn lover, expresses a note of foreboding in his preference for a horn, with its pun on the cuckold's horn. In order to be cuckolded, Benedick would have to be married — hence, to love. When, later in the scene, he has been tricked into falling in love, he continues to use soldier's terms; he prepares himself for the probability that wit will be "broken" and "paper bullets" will be spent on him in his new role.

Claudio, commenting on Benedick as the victim of the deceit, refers to him as "kid-fox," "fowl" to be stalked, and "fish" to be hooked. Benedick is to be tricked as animals are tricked by men in their hunting sports. Benedick is also seen as the unwary victim of love's "infection" — a disease image.

Don Pedro comments that Benedick is as brave as Hector, and he wishes the "same net spread" for Beatrice as for Benedick. He thus continues the military and animal imagery in relation to Benedick.

Finally, Beatrice continues the association of Benedick with the animal kingdom (he is, in effect, a "daw"), with food (he has no "stomach"), and with the military (he may take as much pleasure in her calling him to dinner as can fit on a "knife's point").

ACT III · SCENE 1

Summary

Hero enters Leonato's garden accompanied by her two gentlewomen, Ursula and Margaret. Hero tells Margaret to go to Beatrice, who is talking with the Prince and Claudio, and inform her that she and Ursula are talking about her in the garden. Margaret must also tell Beatrice to "steal into the pleachèd bower," where she will be able to overhear the conversation. After Margaret leaves, Hero instructs Ursula to praise Benedick whenever his name is mentioned. Hero will talk about how "sick in love with Beatrice" Benedick is.

Beatrice enters, observed by Hero, and the two girls begin their deception. As they walk near Beatrice's hiding place, Hero says that Beatrice is "too disdainful" and her spirits are as wild as the "haggerds" (hawks) of the rocks. Ursula asks Hero if she is sure that Benedick truly loves Beatrice. Hero replies it is certain because the Prince and Claudio told her. Even though they asked her to inform Beatrice of Benedick's affection, Hero persuaded them to let Benedick "wrestle with affection" rather than let Beatrice know of it. After all, Hero points out, "Nature never framed a woman's heart / Of prouder stuff than that of Beatrice." In her eyes there are always "disdain" and "scorn." Ursula agrees that Beatrice would probably make fun of Benedick's love if she knew of it. Hero reiterates Beatrice's contrary nature concerning men. She always "spells" a man "backward" (that is, distorts his good features), no matter how many remarkable attributes he may have. For example, to Beatrice a "fair-faced" man is too pretty, and a dark-complexioned man is Nature's "foul blot;" a tall man is a lance with a round head, and a short man is only a miniature, carved imitation; an articulate man is a weather vane blown about by the winds, and a silent man is nothing but a block of stone. In this manner, says Hero, Beatrice turns "...every man the wrong side out." Ursula remarks that such "carping is not commendable." Hero agrees, but she is afraid to tell Beatrice this because her cousin would then "mock me into air" and "press me to death with wit!" It is better to let Benedick pine away than reveal his love, lest he die from mockery. Ursula begs Hero to tell Beatrice, but Hero is firm. She says she will go to Benedick and try to dissuade him from loving Beatrice by fashioning some "honest slanders" against her (that is, appropriate "slanders" which will not throw doubt on her virtue). Perhaps this will "poison" Benedick against Beatrice. Ursula objects to this because Benedick is a "rare gentleman" and Beatrice, who is supposed to have wit and discernment, could not possibly reject him. Hero remarks that indeed Benedick is "the only man of Italy," Claudio excepted, of course. Ursula goes even beyond this description by stating that Benedick "For shape, for bearing, argument and valor,/Goes foremost in report through Italy." Ursula playfully asks Hero when she will be married, and Hero answers every day, after tomorrow. As they leave, the two girls swear that Beatrice has been caught like a bird.

After they have gone, Beatrice comes out from hiding. She is upset by the "fire in mine ears," or rather, the talk that has made her ears burn. She has heard that she stands, "condemned for pride and scorn." She bids contempt and maiden pride farewell. She immediately decides that a contemptuous maiden's reputation is far from glorious: "No glory hides behind the back of such." She vows to let her wild heart be tamed by Benedick's "loving hand," and to return the love he has for her. Beatrice now believes that Benedick is a most deserving man.

Commentary

This scene provides a parallel to the preceding scene, in which the men deceived the eavesdropping Benedick. It also provides the climax of the first part of the plot against the two scoffers by fulfilling the expectation that they would be brought to love each other. With Beatrice now converted, all that remains is for the two lovers to find a way to admit their mutual love.

Hero's remark that she will slander Beatrice to Benedick is an ironical anticipation of the slander that is about to be committed against herself through Don John and Borachio.

In addition, the scene continues to fill in the interval of time between the announcement of the wedding of Hero and Claudio and the actual ceremony and prepares for a double wedding.

Obediently participating in the conspiracy against her cousin, Hero shows that she can play the game of deceit as well as any. She speaks up and reveals a humorous side that is delightful.

Emerging again as the proud and self-centered creature who is yet (due to her sensitivity) susceptible to the insinuation that Benedick loves her, Beatrice does not huff and puff about her new-found love as Benedick does. Rather, she goes into a flight of passion, which is conveyed in rhyme that suggests in its form the last part of a sonnet.

Blank verse is used throughout this scene, except for twelve lines that are spoken, first in a rhyming couplet by Hero, then in the form of the final ten lines of a (Shakespearean type) sonnet by Beatrice. The rhythm scheme is *ababcdcdee*. Thus the effect of Beatrice's conversion is heightened and made more artificial than the scene of Benedick's betrayal.

The language also is more artificial in this scene than in the preceding one. The total effect is more imaginative and more lofty.

The images here parallel those in the previous scene. Both Hero and Ursula use images from the areas of sports and animal life to suggest the way they are deceiving their victim. Hero mentions the "sweet bait we lay" for fish and the "traps" she and her co-conspirators employ. Ursula speaks of "angling" and of trapping (Beatrice is "limed"). Both Hero and Ursula see Beatrice as devouring the bait held out to her.

Beatrice decides she will tame her own "wild heart," which like a bird has been shy and reluctant.

ACT III · SCENE 2

Summary

Don Pedro, Claudio, Benedick, and Leonato enter Leonato's house a short while after the preceding scene. Don Pedro informs them he will leave for Arragon after Claudio is married. Claudio offers to accompany Don Pedro, but the Prince refuses his offer because it would ruin Claudio's honeymoon. Instead, Don Pedro says he will ask Benedick to accompany him, for Benedick is always good for a joke or witty remark. Benedick quietly answers, "Gallants, I am not as I have been." Benedick's three companions take this remark as a signal for them to begin teasing him.

Leonato remarks that Benedick looks "sadder," and Claudio voices the hope that his friend is in love. Don Pedro quickly observes that Benedick would be a traitor if he *were* in love. Benedick pretends to have a toothache, and Don Pedro tells him to "draw" it. Benedick is provoked now and says "hang it!" whereupon Claudio informs him that it must be hanged first and drawn afterwards. Benedick states that their advice is a waste of time because "everyone can master a grief but he that has it." Claudio still insists that Benedick is in love. Don Pedro jestingly remarks that Benedick shows no signs of love, unless it is a love of "strange disguises." He says that Benedick has taken to wearing different kinds of clothing each day. It "appears" he has a "fancy to this foolery." Claudio still insists that Benedick is in love because all the signs point to it: he now brushes his hat every morning and he has finally gone to the barber to have his beard removed (the whiskers have already "stuffed tennis balls"). Don Pedro says that Benedick is wearing "civet" (perfume) and that he looks rather melancholy. Claudio jokingly asks when Benedick was ever so concerned about keeping his face clean. They even notice that he now "paints himself." (This refers to the custom of men using cosmetics.) They are forced to the inevitable conclusion that he is in love. Thus, the woman, whom they know loves him, will "die" for him (the word "die" had at that time a slang meaning implying the sexual act).

All of this is too much for Benedick, so he asks Leonato to step aside with him for a short conversation. Don Pedro and Claudio are certain Benedick is going to talk to Leonato about Beatrice.

"John the Bastard" enters and requests a private audience with Don Pedro, even though he says Claudio may hear what he has to say. Don John slyly asks Claudio if he plans to be married tomorrow, and Don Pedro says he knows he is. Don John replies that Claudio may not wish to be married after learning what Don John knows. Claudio asks what the "impediment" could be. Don John replies that, even though Claudio thinks he does not love him, his service will now demonstrate the friendship he has for the young count. He tells Claudio that Hero is disloyal. But that word is too gentle to describe her, he adds. If Don Pedro and Claudio will accompany him, they will see her meeting with a lover, and "her chamber window entered" tonight, the very night before her marriage. They do not want to believe that such a thing could be possible, but Don John tells them to wait until they have seen it with their own eyes. Claudio swears that if this terrible information is true, he will shame Hero in the very congregation where he was to be married to her. In addition, Don Pedro says he will join with Claudio in disgracing her if she is untrue. They leave, each voicing his shock at the turn of events. Don John remarks that he has done them a great service.

Commentary

The Benedick-Beatrice plot moves one more step ahead with Benedick now exhibiting all the marks of a lover. His conference with Leonato, supposedly on the subject of Beatrice, prepares for the eventual double wedding.

Don John's scheme against Hero and Claudio also moves ahead, changing the gay mood to a sinister, foreboding one. An element of suspense is introduced as to whether Claudio will disgrace Hero publicly if he discovers her in a compromising position. Claudio's speech concerning the death that comes to a woman who loves a hard-hearted man (i.e., Benedick) ironically hints at the "death" of Hero as a result of Claudio's own hard-heartedness.

The scene also prepares for Don Pedro's departure to Arragon immediately after the wedding (far sooner than he had indicated to Leonato in Act I, Scene 1).

Although Benedick indicates that he has assumed a strange new role — that of the lover — he is the same impressionable soul that he has been. He has adopted the stylish manner of lovers, both in mood and in fashion of dress, yet the wilfulness and determination to play his chosen role, come what may, have always been characteristic of him.

The childish dependence of Claudio is suggested, not only by his general relationship to Don Pedro (he offers, while on his honeymoon, to accompany the Prince part of the way home!), but by the words with which the Prince refuses the youth's offer to accompany him towards Arragon: "Nay, that would be as great a soil in the new gloss of your marriage as to show a child a new coat and forbid him to wear it." Claudio and Don Pedro echo each other so frequently that each seems a chorus to the other. Claudio's haste in accepting the idea of Hero's unfaithfulness, and his callousness in threatening to disgrace her publicly, confirm certain impressions he gave earlier. Claudio had been hasty in falling in love and in wanting to be married at once. He had been gullible in imagining that Don Pedro was betraying him at the masque. He had been somewhat callous in his method of wooing (using an intermediary), and in his concern that Hero have a proper dowry.

The Prince displays a certain moodiness in his decision to cut short his visit to Leonato. The ease with which he is persuaded to swallow the story of Hero's affair may suggest reluctance on his part to let Claudio marry (he would be losing a friend). If Hero should turn out to be "loose," she would not be a fit mate for Claudio, who could then remain single and continue in the Prince's retinue. Don Pedro is as callous as Claudio in agreeing to disgrace the presumably tainted Hero at the wedding.

Used throughout this scene, prose illuminates the difference between Don John and the other characters. Claudio, Don Pedro, and Benedick adopt much the same figurative style, and in this scene the style is rather staccato in the short speeches. Don John's prose remains the antithetical, balanced, artificial vehicle of a disturbed mind attempting to control itself. "I could say she were worse; think you of a worse title, and I will fit her to it. Wonder not till further warrant" gives an accurate idea of Don John's style as a conspirator.

Claudio uses animal, music, and sports imagery to ridicule the new lover, Benedick. Don Pedro, with his reference to wedding bells, his scoffs at the disguises lovers assume (clothing imagery), and his reference to the myth of Cupid, continues the joke at Benedick's expense. And Don John resorts to an image of tailoring (clothing) to indicate his role as an active manipulator of Hero's reputation.

ACT III · SCENE 3

Summary

This scene takes place later that night in a street not far from Leonato's house. Dogberry the constable, Verges the headborough (a less important officer), and two members of the watch (similar to policemen) enter. Dogberry is preparing to "charge" the watch (that is, give them their instructions). Dogberry asks if they are "good men and true" and learns from Verges that they are, "or else it were pity but they should suffer salvation, body and soul." Dogberry answers that "salvation" would be too good a punishment for their having any "allegiance in them."

We soon realize that these characters are the low, or comic, characters. Not only do they have a particular way of speaking, but they also slaughter the English language with remarkable ease. Dogberry appoints one of the members of the watch to be the temporary constable because, not only can he read and write, but he is also "thought here to be the most senseless and fit man for the constable of the watch." Dogberry then proceeds to give them their orders: "you shall comprehend all vagrom men; you are to bid any man stand, in the Prince's name." And if the man won't halt? "Why then, take no note of him, but let him go" and then thank God you are "rid of a knave," says Dogberry. Also, the watch should not make any noise, adds Dogberry, for it is "most tolerable and not to be endured" for the watch to babble. The watch agrees that they would rather sleep than talk anyway, and Dogberry finds no harm in that. They should also make the rounds of the alehouses and bid those who are drunk to go home to bed. If they refuse to go, says Dogberry, then the watch should "let them alone till they are sober." Dogberry then informs them that if they meet a thief they can suspect him "to be no true man." The less they meddle with such men, the better it will be for them. But, ask the watch, can they not lay hands on a thief? They are certainly permitted to do so, says Dogberry, but it is his opinion that "they that touch pitch will be defiled." It is best to let a thief "steal out of your company." Dogberry astounds the members of the watch by telling them they can even stop the Prince if they meet up with him. Verges thinks they cannot do that, but Dogberry is willing to bet "five shillings to one on't." Of course, the Prince must be willing, for the watch should offend no man. Verges agrees with this logic, and Dogberry leaves.

The members of the watch prepare to sit upon a bench until two o'clock and then go home to bed. Dogberry returns and tells them to pay special attention to Leonato's house because of the marriage tomorrow. He leaves them with the command: "Be vigitant, I beseech you."

Conrade and Borachio enter, and the members of the watch hide in order to overhear Borachio's tale. Borachio informs Conrade that he has earned one thousand ducats from Don John for performing a villainous deed. Borachio, probably having had too much to drink, gets sidetracked momentarily on the subject of fashion and how clothing cannot "make the man" or hide a villain. He then tells Conrade how he has just wooed Margaret who, dressed in her mistress' clothes, pretended she was Hero. He says that, as he was doing this, Don John, who had already set the scene, led Claudio and Don Pedro to a vantage point where they could see the "amiable encounter." Conrade guesses immediately that they thought Margaret was Hero. Borachio says that, due to Don John's oath and the darkness, Claudio left furious, swearing that he would shame her the next morning in church by sending her home "without a husband."

At this point the first and second watch jump out from hiding and arrest Conrade and Borachio. The second watch decides to call Dogberry because they have "recovered the most dangerous piece of lechery that ever was known in the commonwealth." (Of course the word "treachery" is meant not "lechery.") Conrade and Borachio go off meekly with the watch as Conrade voices the opinion that they will indeed look foolish, having been arrested by such fools.

Commentary

The introduction of the subplot of the watch — a satire on the law enforcement of the day — prepares for the uncovering of Don John's scheme. The exposure of the plot, in a sense the climax of the play, builds further suspense, for although the audience is now assured that Claudio and the Prince will learn the truth about Hero, the question arises as to whether or not they will learn it before the wedding.

The mock-serious instructions of Dogberry and Verges to the watch offer a broad contrast to the preceding scenes, which have been witty and serious, but not so broadly humorous. Dogberry's pomposity introduces a new and farcical dimension to the play. His malapropisms (misuse of words) and his sense of self-sufficiency create an atmosphere all his own. It is ironical that the blundering ignorance of the watch will prove the undoing of Don John's plot. Ignorance is often more successful than careful cunning.

The dialogue between Borachio and Conrade on the subject of fashion stresses the theme of appearance and reality.

A type of rustic clown that Shakespeare liked to present,

Dogberry is full of self-importance in the pursuit of his duties as constable. His pomposity is only matched by his expertise in the use of malapropisms: "First, who think you the most desartless [deserving] man to be constable?" Being peace-loving and kindly, Dogberry is an endearing oaf.

The co-constable, Verges, is talkative and coins his own malapropisms: "Yea, or else it were pity but they should suffer salvation [damnation], body and soul." He can be peppery and argumentative. He and Dogberry make an apt pair.

Borachio, Don John's cohort, is unable to hold his whiskey or his tongue. His talkativeness indicates that he is self-defeating; he invites his own capture.

The language, prose throughout, is marked by the malapropisms of Dogberry and the watch. "Salvation" is used for "damnation," "desartless" for "deserving," and so on. There is also naïve double meaning in various words like "stand" and "meddle."

The imagery here is concerned principally with fashion. Borachio drunkenly muses over the way in which fashion and clothes tend to change young persons into what they are not, "sometime fashioning them like Pharoah's soldiers in the reechy painting, sometime like god Bel's priests in the old church window, sometime like the shaven Hercules in the smirched worm-eaten tapestry, where his codpiece seems as massy as his club...." The mention of Hercules picks up a recurrent motif in the play: Hercules as the doer of wonders, Hercules as the pawn of Juno and the slave of Omphale, and, here, Hercules as the victim of an extravagant artistic conception. The point of the last allusion to Hercules is that the clothes do not matter; it is the man underneath who counts.

It is Borachio's metaphor of fashion as a "thief" that warns the watch of villainy afoot. A person's true nature may be stolen away from him by the robes he wears. High or low, aristocratic or menial, he is made what he is by his appearance, Borachio suggests.

ACT III · SCENE 4

Summary

The scene is a room in Leonato's house on the day of the wedding. Hero and Margaret are preparing Hero's wedding garments. Hero sends Ursula to wake Beatrice so she may help her dress.

Beatrice enters in a drowsy, subdued fashion and Hero asks: "Why, how now? Do you speak in the sick tune?" Beatrice answers, "I am out of all other tune, methinks." Margaret and Hero begin teasing Beatrice about her having fallen in love. Margaret suggests that, since Beatrice is in a "sick tune," they should all sing "Light o' Love." Beatrice again remarks that she is "exceeding ill" and Margaret questions her: "For a hawk, a horse, or a husband?" Beatrice cleverly

evades the issue by answering: "For the letter that begins them all, H."
(She is punning on the pronunciation of the letter "H" — aitch —
which probably was sounded as "ache.")

Beatrice remarks that she is "stuffed" (that is, she is congested).
Margaret does not let that go by without a suggestive remark: "A
maid, and stuffed! There's goodly catching of cold." (She refers to
pregnancy.) Margaret suggests that Beatrice take some "distilled *Cardius Benedictus*" and lay it to her heart. (*Cardius Benedictus*, known
as "blessed" or "holy thistle," was a medicinal herb.) Beatrice asks
why Margaret has suggested a medicine with the name "Benedictus,"
and if there is any "moral" in the implication. Margaret answers that
there could not be any moral. No indeed. She knows better than to
think Beatrice could ever fall in love. Benedick was the same kind of
person once and, now that he is in love, things are not much different
for him: he still "eats his meat without grudging." Perhaps, Margaret
adds, Beatrice may also be converted to normal behavior: "But
methinks you look with your eyes as other women do."

Ursula enters and breathlessly exclaims that the Prince, Claudio,
Benedick, Don John "and all the gallants of the town are come to
fetch you to church." The girls quickly run off to help Hero dress for
her wedding.

Commentary

This scene parallels the second scene in this act by showing that
Beatrice is just as love-sick as Benedick, and thoroughly enjoying her
misery. Beatrice's somewhat affected melancholy provides a humorous
counterpoint to Hero's moodiness. Hero's anxious state and her
fussiness over the wedding clothes contribute to the sense that some
tragic event is in the making. Hero's mood is also counterpointed by
Margaret's jokes, which suggest a coarser side of her nature than has
hitherto been revealed.

The theme of appearance and reality is further developed through
the disagreements among the ladies as to which wedding garments
Hero will wear. Since appearances are deceiving, people commit errors
of judgment. Hero's preoccupation with appearances arouses the audience's sympathy, for appearances have been the means by which
Borachio and Don John have undermined her reputation in the eyes of
Claudio and Don Pedro.

The bride-to-be is moodier than might have been expected. But
still waters run deep. She shows herself aloof, and even prim, in
response to Margaret's off-color joke about the sex relationship that
will follow marriage. But when Margaret flatters her taste in clothes,
Hero brightens up. Perhaps she is dwelling too much on fashion and
appearances.

In an attempt to shake her lady out of depression, Margaret

makes an indecent reference to the consummation of the marriage. This coarseness implies the nature that could have participated in Borachio's intrigue against Hero. Margaret's part in the proceedings apparently has not made her feel guilty. She therefore acts quite naturally in assisting Hero prepare for the wedding that ironically she has helped sabotage.

ACT III · SCENE 5

Summary

Dogberry and Verges have called upon Leonato with some information. Even though Leonato displays his impatience, Dogberry and Verges are absolutely unable to get to the point, or even make sense. Leonato is pressed beyond endurance and finally blurts out his impatience. Of course, Dogberry misunderstands what Leonato has said and goes off on a new tangent:

> **Leonato:** Neighbors, you are tedious.
>
> **Dogberry:** It pleases your worship to say so but we are the poor Duke's officers; but truly, for mine own part, if I were as tedious as a king, I could find in my heart to bestow it all of your worship.
>
> **Leonato:** All thy tediousness on me, ha?
>
> **Dogberry:** Yea, and 'twere a thousand pounds more than 'tis; for I hear as good exclamation on your worship as of any man in the city, and though I be but a poor man, I am glad to hear it.

Finally, only after Leonato threatens to leave, does Dogberry inform him that the watch has "comprehended two aspicious persons" and that the two officers would like Leonato to examine them. Leonato tells them of his haste, orders them to examine the men themselves and bring him the report, offers them some wine, and finally rushes off to give his daughter away in marriage. The two conscientious peacekeepers leave "to examination these men."

Commentary

The scene shows that the watch have properly followed up their responsibility in reporting the capture of Borachio and Conrade. The dawdling self-importance of Dogberry and Verges contrasts with the seriousness of Leonato, whose haste to go to his daughter's wedding prevents him from paying as much attention to the watch as he should, thus causing a minor crisis in the play. If Leonato had listened, Don John's plan would have been foiled. As a result of Leonato's failure to listen, the audience continues to feel suspense as to what exactly will happen at the church. The final effect of the scene is to provide a humorous lull before the storm.

Dogberry is too pompous to blurt out his story, and too vain to let Verges get credit for telling it. Verges, also, is self-important and rather childishly competitive. Though intending to be courteous to his law officers, Leonato feels impelled to hurry to church for his daughter's wedding. The practical requirements of law enforcement yield to the practical requirements of domestic responsibility. However, he does order the constable to carry out the examination, and he is considerate enough to offer the men wine.

This scene, in prose, is notable for Dogberry's mistaken and humorous vocabulary. The exchange between Leonato and Dogberry quoted in the Summary, is typical.

ACT IV · SCENE 1

Summary

All the major characters, as well as attendants and various townsmen, are present in the church. Leonato tells the friar to marry Claudio and Hero first, and give them the obligatory personal instructions afterwards. When the friar asks Claudio if he knows of any "inward impediment" which would prevent the marriage, Leonato boldly answers "none" for Claudio.

Claudio objects to the answer and makes a great show of returning Hero, "this rotten orange," to her father. He accuses her of having known the "heat of a luxurious bed." Her blushes are signs of guilt, not innocence. Hero, speechless, cannot answer the charge. Leonato thinks that perhaps Claudio has already taken her virginity and is now accusing her of being unchaste. Claudio says that this is not the case, but that Hero is an immoral woman. Leonato asks why Don Pedro is silent, and Don Pedro replies: "What should I speak?/I stand dishonored that have gone about/To link my dear friend to a common stale." Benedick remarks with biting irony, "This looks not like a nuptial," and Claudio asks Leonato to command Hero to answer truthfully. Leonato does so, and Claudio asks Hero what man it was she talked with last night between twelve and one. Hero replies that she talked with no man at that hour. Don Pedro then recounts the previous night's vigil at which they saw "a ruffian at her chamber window" who revealed the many "vile encounters they have had/A thousand times in secret." Don John corroborates the story, but says that Hero's evil deeds are too offensive to be uttered.

Claudio then accuses Hero of only pretending to be pure. He swears that he will never again fall in love, and that his thoughts will henceforth be full of suspicion. Leonato calls for someone to end his life on the spot. Hero faints from shock, and, on the advice of Don John, the three accusers leave.

Benedick and Beatrice attempt to look after Hero, but Leonato wishes for Hero's death. He cries out that he is sorry he loved her so dearly and took pride in her. In fact, Leonato, thinking that Hero is dying, says that if she should revive he might even kill her. The friar tells Leonato that he has studied Hero's character and, from the anguish and blushes in her face, has concluded she is innocent. Hero swears that she talked with no one last night, and the friar realizes there has been a terrible misunderstanding. Benedick immediately notes that if Don Pedro and Claudio's "wisdoms be misled in this,/The practice of it lives in John the bastard,/Whose spirits toil in frame of villainies." Leonato swears to be avenged upon them if they have spoken falsely.

But the friar suggests a plan whereby Leonato will give out the news that Hero has died of shame. Then, in one of the finest poetic speeches in the play, the friar tells Leonato that this deception will give Claudio pause to think about how beautiful Hero's life was:

> Th' idea of her life shall sweetly creep
> Into his study of imagination,
> And every lovely organ [feature] of her life
> Shall come apparelled in more precious habit,
> More moving, delicate, and full of life,
> Into the eye and prospect of his soul
> Than when she lived indeed.

Claudio will mourn for her and perhaps the truth will be known soon. In any case, the manner of her death will wipe away her shame. But, as a last resort, if the deception does not turn out for the best, Hero can enter a convent. Benedick promises to help Leonato in this trick even though he owes allegiance to Don Pedro and Claudio. Leonato agrees to the friar's plan. Everyone leaves, except Beatrice and Benedick. Beatrice is crying, and Benedick is upset by her tears. He boldly declares his love and she replies with possibly too much coyness:

> **Benedick:** I do love nothing in the world as well as you. Is not that strange?
>
> **Beatrice:** As strange as the thing I know not. It were as possible for me to say I loved nothing so well as you. But believe me not; and yet I lie not. I confess nothing, nor I deny nothing. I am sorry for my cousin.

But finally Benedick forces Beatrice to admit her love for him. In a very famous exchange of lines, Beatrice not only declares her love for Benedick, but creates a new direction in the play.

Beatrice: Will you not eat your word?

Benedick: With no sauce that can be devised to it. I protest I love thee.

Beatrice: Why then, God forgive me!

Benedick: What offence, sweet Beatrice?

Beatrice: You have stayed me in a happy hour. I was about to protest I loved you.

Benedick: And do it with all thy heart.

Beatrice: I love you with so much of my heart that none is left to protest.

Benedick: Come, bid me do anything for thee.

Beatrice: Kill Claudio.

Benedick: Ha! Not for the wide world!

Beatrice: You kill me to deny it. Farewell.

Benedick detains her. Yet she is insistent about Claudio and furious over his slandering Hero in public. She uses the feminine trick of accusing Benedick of not loving her and being a coward for not fighting against her enemy. Benedick finally quiets her and asks if she really believes in her soul that "Count Claudio hath wronged Hero." She says she is certain, and Benedick decides that he will challenge Claudio in order to avenge the honor of Beatrice's cousin. He sends Beatrice to comfort her cousin and leaves to spread the word of Hero's death.

Commentary

Three of the main plots in the play come to a head in this climactic scene. Claudio's plan to marry Hero has been thwarted by Don John's slander of her character. Thus Claudio, instead of marrying Hero, denounces her at her wedding.

The Claudio-Hero plot receives another twist, however, as a result of Hero's swoon. Friar Francis at this point originates a plot that is based on the assumption that Hero is innocent.

Don John's plot also reaches its climax here. When Claudio denounces and abandons Hero, he brings shame and humiliation upon Leonato's family, upon Hero and himself, and upon proper society in general. The audience, however, aware that the watch has caught Borachio and Conrade, knows that the revelation of the truth is at hand.

The final plot is that of Benedick and Beatrice. This is the first time that the two have been alone since they were tricked. The catastrophe that has overtaken Hero serves to bind Benedick and

Beatrice together. Their loyalty to Hero stands in marked contrast with Leonato's doubt. But at the end of the scene, the Benedick-Beatrice plot reaches its climax and takes a new turn. Upon hearing Benedick's confession of love, Beatrice demands that he kill Claudio. A new threat thus enters the situation. Benedick, in challenging Claudio, may introduce bloodshed into the play.

Suspense arises because of the number of questions to be solved: How will Claudio react to the news of Hero's supposed death? How will the revelations of the watch affect the working-out of Friar Francis' plan? Will Benedick challenge Claudio? If so, what will come of it? Thus, this scene not only serves as a climax, but it introduces a number of new complications to be resolved.

Leonato, the doting father, is eager to have the wedding proceed and so he readily answers questions put to Claudio and Hero. At Hero's disgrace, he is embarrassed, vengeful and vindictive. He has little choice but to believe the Prince. Yet, while melancholy, he has enough faith in his daughter to see the practicality and fairness of Friar Francis' plan.

At the exposure of Hero, the friar shows that, as a man of broad experience, he is discerning enough to trust in Hero's innocence. Sympathetic to Hero, he remains the only reasonable person in the group, and devises an ingenious plan to redeem Hero and perhaps restore her in Claudio's affections.

In disgracing Hero publicly, Claudio shows a petty, vain, impulsive streak. Having made a vow with the Prince to humiliate his intended bride, he is obsessive enough to carry it out to the letter. His loyalty to Don Pedro is thus greater than his love for Hero. Despite good cause, his wilfullness appears extreme.

Hero's swoon, and the way in which she blushes on recovery, suggest her innocence of spirit. It is not in her nature to stand up to brutal treatment; she tends to retreat into herself.

The cruel demand that Benedick kill Claudio in order to retain her love is startlingly in character, for Beatrice. She has always been vindictive towards men, and this demand on Benedick is consistent with her previous image as a sort of Ate (Fury).

The witty Benedick is intuitive enough to realize that the villainous slanderer must be Don John. His timidity at first keeps him from expressing his love for Beatrice; it also, later, makes him refrain from sending a challenge to Claudio. However, in this conflict between love (for Beatrice) and friendship (for Claudio), love finally wins out.

After the preliminaries to the wedding, which are in prose, the disgrace of Hero and the plan devised by Friar Francis to redeem her name are in poetry (blank verse). This switch to verse heightens the tragic effect of the scene, and lends it a slightly artificial aspect.

Benedick and Beatrice fill the last lines of the scene with their versatile prose repartee. This verbal fencing (stichomythia) is in marked contrast to the previous tragic action.

ACT IV · SCENE 2

Summary

Dressed in their robes of office, Dogberry, Verges and the sexton (town clerk), accompanied by the members of the watch, enter the prison to examine the prisoners. The sexton asks, "Which be the malefactors?" and the two bumbling officials answer:

Dogberry: Marry, that am I and my partner.

Verges: Nay, that's certain. We have the exhibition to examine.

After Dogberry creates the initial confusion about the names of the "malefactors," the sexton asks him to call the watch to state the charges. The second watch says that Borachio received a thousand ducats from Don John for "accusing the Lady Hero wrongfully." The first watch reveals that Claudio, acting on the strength of the accusation and deception, planned to disgrace Hero and not marry her. When Dogberry hears this, all he can say is: "O villain! Thou wilt be condemned into everlasting redemption for this." The sexton notes that the charges are indeed proven by the facts. Prince John has fled secretly this morning; Hero was accused exactly as stated, and died from grief. The sexton orders that the prisoners be bound. He leaves to bring the examination to Leonato's house, and tells Dogberry to convey the prisoners there also. Conrade loses his patience and says to Dogberry: "Away! You are an ass, you are an ass." Dogberry is infuriated by this and flies into a passion:

Dost thou not suspect my place? Dost thou not suspect my years? O that he were here to write me down an ass! But, masters, remember that I am an ass. Though it be not written down, yet forget not that I am an ass...O that I had been writ down an ass!

Of course, what Dogberry means is he wishes the sexton were present so it could be recorded officially that the prisoner called him an ass. They take the prisoners away.

Commentary

This scene moves the plot of the watch forward one step in the partial interrogation of Borachio and Conrade. The two blunderers,

Dogberry and Verges, provide comic relief from the serious scene that has preceded this one.

The binding-over of the prisoners for further questioning by the Governor, Leonato, is a necessary stage in proving the innocence of Hero, implicating Don John, and releasing Benedick from his obligation to kill Claudio. Don John's flight prepares for the eventuality that he will be caught and punished for his wickedness. The scene also indicates that Friar Francis' plan is being carried out, for it has become known that Hero is dead.

The constable reaps a just reward for his incompetence by being called a "coxcomb" and an "ass." Thoroughly frustrated at being ignored and being called names, Dogberry reaches heights of absurd indignation. Though he should let the insults be forgotten, he continues to remind everyone that he has been called an ass. Perhaps this is the only comfort he can salvage from the proceedings. At least he has that much claim to the center of the stage.

The prose of this scene is thick with Dogberry's malapropisms and misunderstandings. When it is revealed that Borachio called Don John a villain, Dogberry exclaims, "Why, this flat perjury, to call a prince's brother villain;" and when it is testified that Borachio has received a thousand ducats for accusing Hero wrongfully, Dogberry bursts out, "Flat burglary as ever was committed."

Assured that the prisoners are villains, Dogberry cries, "Come, let them be opinioned" a word that recalls *opinion*, suggesting the give-and-take of the testimony to be given at Leonato's, and *pinions* the irons that are to bind the prisoners. It is likely that the sexton's suggestion that "these men be bound" is interpreted by Dogberry to mean *literally* bound rather than "bound over for trial." Hence the richness of the word "opinioned."

That Dogberry misunderstands what others are saying is apparent when the sexton asks who are the "malefactors." Dogberry replies, "Marry, that am I and my partner." As if to atone for his failure to give Leonato an adequate idea of the significance of the prisoners taken into custody, Dogberry here speaks the truth.

ACT V · SCENE 1

Summary

Antonio tries to convince Leonato to forget his anger over Claudio's treatment of Hero. But Leonato is not to be reasoned with. He says that the man who is not suffering a grief finds it easy to tell others to be patient: "No, no! 'Tis all men's office to speak patience/To those that wring under the load of sorrow." As long as he is feeling the emotional pain caused by the loss of his honor, Leonato cannot be stoical: "For there was never yet philosopher/That could endure the toothache patiently." Antonio advises Leonato to save some of his anger to use against his offenders. Don Pedro and Claudio enter. Leonato tries to speak to them, but Don Pedro wishes to leave quickly. Leonato becomes angry at the slight, and accuses Claudio of having wronged him and his child. Of course, Claudio does not believe that he has committed any villainy. Leonato challenges him to a duel but Claudio refuses to fight with him. At this point Antonio loses his temper and hurls abuse at Claudio: "Come, follow me, boy. Come, sir boy, come follow me./Sir boy, I'll whip you from your foining fence!/Nay, as I am a gentleman, I will."

Leonato is unable to quiet his brother. Finally Don Pedro insists that Hero's guilt was proved. He refuses to listen any further to the two outraged brothers. They leave, swearing they will be heard. Benedick enters, and his two friends inform him that he almost witnessed a terrible battle between the old and the young. But Benedick speaks little to them and refuses to respond to their jests. Finally, he takes Claudio aside and challenges him to a duel. He tells Claudio that he will inform the town of his cowardice if Claudio refuses to fight. Don Pedro tries to tease Benedick further by telling him of the funny remarks Beatrice made about him the other day. Before Benedick leaves, he notifies Don Pedro that he must discontinue their friendship:

> My lord, for your many courtesies I thank you. I must discontinue your company. Your brother the bastard is fled from Messina. You have among you killed a sweet and innocent lady. For my Lord Lackbeard there, he and I shall meet; and till then peace be with him.

Don Pedro realizes that Benedick speaks in earnest. He and Claudio agree that Benedick's actions are a result of his love for Beatrice. At this point, Dogberry, Verges and the members of the watch enter, dragging Conrade and Borachio, who are bound. Don Pedro has become alarmed by the news of his brother's sudden disappearance from Messina. He asks Dogberry why Don John's men are bound. Of course, Dogberry is unable to make any sense, so Don Pedro is finally required to question the captives himself. Borachio then confesses everything to Don Pedro and Claudio. Don Pedro and the young count are horrified by the news:

> **Don Pedro:** Runs not this speech like iron through your blood?
>
> **Claudio:** I have drunk poison whiles he uttered it.

Leonato and Antonio enter with the sexton. Leonato wishes to see the man who has caused the death of his innocent child. Yet Leonato does not assign all the blame to Borachio. He also accuses Don Pedro and Claudio of having played their part. Claudio is stricken with remorse, and swears he will carry out any penance Leonato wishes to impose on him. Don Pedro also begs Leonato's forgiveness. Leonato asks them both to inform the inhabitants of Messina of the exact truth about Hero's death. He requires Claudio to "hang her an epitaph upon her tomb" and to marry his brother's daughter in place of Hero. Claudio agrees to marry Leonato's niece in the morning. Borachio explains that Margaret did not know that she was used in a wicked deception. Dogberry breaks in and reminds Leonato to punish "this plaintiff here, the offender" (Conrade) for having called him an ass. Dogberry rants on about how hard it is for people to borrow money lately. Leonato takes the hint, and throws a purse of money to Dogberry who, overjoyed, literally bows and scrapes his way out, muttering complete nonsense in praise of Leonato. The others announce they will meet in the morning (at church). Claudio and the Prince decide to visit Hero's tomb.

Commentary

This scene further develops Leonato as the hasty, emotional father by dramatizing the extravagance of his reaction to his daughter's disgrace. Shakespeare thus prepares the audience for Leonato's triumph in the last scene. Up to this point in the play, Don Pedro, and then Friar Francis, have controlled the action. Now Shakespeare is ready for Leonato to assume the role of leader. It is to Leonato, as Governor of Messina, that the watch brings the prisoners; and it is he who carries out and improves upon Friar Francis' plot. By displaying great emotion Leonato so overwhelms Claudio and the Prince that the melancholy youth agrees to do penance at Hero's tomb and to enter into a rather absurd marriage to the old man's "niece". The fact that Antonio goes so much further than Leonato in angry denunciation of the youthful Claudio establishes him as a type of angry old man, and increases the sympathy for Leonato as the more restrained of the two. Sympathy is also won for Claudio as the object of two challenges and as the penitent who wishes to atone for his error in accusing Hero, who has been restored in his and Don Pedro's eyes. Benedick, too, wins the audience's sympathy as one who, in order to please his beloved, feels duty-bound to challenge a friend. The irony of this challenge lies partly in the fact that, of the two, only Benedick knows that Hero is still alive, and partly in the fact that Benedick does *not* know that she is about to be proven innocent.

Some of the doubts in the mind of the audience over the role of Margaret are cleared up in this scene. Leonato's determination to look into her part in the conspiracy makes it certain that she will receive treatment which is consistent with her guilt.

Because of the challenges offered by Antonio and Benedick, the scene is full of tension. The tension is released by the constables' sudden appearance, which changes the course of the action toward reconciliation. By the end of the scene, the emotions of the audience have been sufficiently aroused to allow them to accept the extraordinary events of the final act.

Claudio possesses the tact and good sense not to fight an old man who challenges him. When his friend, Benedick, issues a similar challenge, he sensibly tries to turn it aside with wit. Although he shows remorse for the wrong done Hero, his promise to do penance at Hero's grave and to marry Leonato's niece are perhaps more calculated to impress the Prince and create a good opinion than to give evidence of meaningful inner change. Claudio remains the superficial upstart soldier of fortune who has learned something, but not much, from his experience.

Leonato's swing from melancholy to anger is perhaps evidence of his instability. More probably, however, it is simply his way of coming to terms with his real feelings. Spurred by Antonio, he denounces Claudio, but at the end of the exchange, it is he who must restrain Antonio. He is thus the more reasonable of the two. Leonato's courteous and effective management of the watch, and of the offending Claudio and Don Pedro, reinforces the sense of his merit. He remains the practical father with a daughter to marry off to an eligible young man. His assurances to Claudio that the "niece" will be provided with a more than adequate dowry show how aware he is of the demands of an arranged marriage.

Practical enough to realize that Leonato's melancholy is unhealthy, Antonio urges his brother to direct his anger at its real cause (Claudio and Don Pedro). Antonio turns out to be more emphatic than Leonato in his demands for justice. Only the restraint of Claudio and the Prince prevent disaster.

Troubled by the conflict between love and friendship, Benedick nevertheless manages to challenge Claudio — a victory of will. His almost obsessive determination is shown, not only in the carrying out of the promise to Beatrice, but in the way in which he keeps from his friends the secret that Hero is really alive.

Pushed aside in an earlier scene by the course of events, Dogberry does his best to restore his authority in the eyes of the aristocrats. His mismanagement of his official position remains consistent but, startlingly enough, Borachio, by confessing his offence, takes the initiative away from the constable. Not to be cheated of his importance, Dogberry ultimately renews his accusations of Conrade for calling him an ass and for referring to "one Deformed." He is materialistic enough to expect a reward, and cunning enough (through flattery and hints) to secure one.

Blank verse is used to express the passionate feelings of Leonato and Antonio and their accusations against Claudio and Don Pedro.

Prose, as usual, is used in situations involving Benedick, and it contrasts with the blank verse of more emotional situations. Dogberry's performance, representative of the lowest social level in the play, likewise is rendered in prose.

ACT V · SCENE 2

Summary

Benedick and Margaret meet in Leonato's garden. Benedick asks her to tell Beatrice he wishes to talk to her. After a witty exchange, Margaret leaves to tell Beatrice. Benedick tries to sing a love song he has composed, but is unable to complete it because it is so inadequate. In a soliloquy, he states that he cannot write about love. Furthermore, he has difficulty finding rhymes: "lady" only rhymes with "baby" — an "innocent rhyme," he says ironically; "scorn" rhymes best with "horn" — "a hard rhyme" to tolerate; and "school" fits best with "fool" — a "babbling rhyme." "No, I was not born under a rhyming planet," he says, "nor I cannot woo in festival terms."

Beatrice enters and asks what has occurred between Benedick and Claudio. Benedick informs her and then changes the subject to how they two fell in love with each other. There is a short, subdued exchange of wit between the two lovers, in which Benedick notes the necessity of building his own monument while he yet lives. (He is referring to a wife and children. Note the anticipation of the next scene in front of Hero's tomb.) Ursula enters and tells them that Don John's plot has been uncovered. Benedick and Beatrice leave to hear the welcome news.

Commentary

This scene fills time until Claudio visits Hero's tomb. It shows Benedick, full of his own virtue for having challenged Claudio, and attempting to adapt to the role of a lover. Still shy, the lovers begin to show a development in their relationship. Benedick's question about Hero's condition reminds the audience that the solidity of the Beatrice-Benedick relationship depends, in part, on their concern for Hero. Suspense continues as to whether Benedick will actually fight with Claudio.

Resuming her role as the witty lady-in-waiting with a flair for the risqué in expression, Margaret reasserts her position in the play. Benedick, in this scene, realizes he is more the soldier than the lover. Beatrice proves clumsy, yet not unpleasing, as the object of Benedick's attentions.

ACT V · SCENE 3

Summary

Claudio and Don Pedro enter the church. They are followed by attendants with candles and musicians. Claudio is shown Leonato's family monument. He takes out a scroll and reads aloud the epitaph he has composed for Hero. The epitaph states that she who was killed by "slanderous tongues" will live "in death with glorious fame." Claudio hangs the scroll on the monument as a memorial to Hero. He then commands the musicians to perform the song composed especially for this occasion. The song states that those who caused Hero's death are deeply repentant. After the song, Claudio swears that he will perform this ritual each year. All the men are given permission to leave, and Don Pedro and Claudio depart to prepare themselves for the upcoming marriage.

Commentary

In carrying out the first of Leonato's requests, Claudio releases a good deal of the tension associated with his brutal treatment of Hero, and wins back the sympathy of the audience.

Providing a contrast with the mood of the preceding action, this scene emphasizes the seriousness of slander, and underlines the motif of hearsay. It also enables the marriage scene that follows to assume the aspect of celebration suitable to a wedding. Penitence is over; joy may resume.

In his determination to make amends for the wrong done to Hero, Claudio establishes a more favorable impression with the audience. Obsessively observing the terms of the penance, he shows a consistent obedience, which has been one of his less agreeable traits. The depth of his feeling is, however, suggested by his resolve to perform this penitential ritual annually.

The poetry here is impressively varied. It sets this scene apart from the rest of the play. In the epitaph (a six-line iambic tetrameter stanza, rhyming *ababcc*), Claudio laments the death of Hero as a result of slander, and prays that she achieve fame in being so wronged. The song (a ten-line stanza, rhyming *aabbccdeed*) is addressed to Diana, goddess of chastity, and begs her pardon for the wrong committed against her follower, Hero. The final ten lines (rhyming *ababcabcbc*) return to iambic pentameter, and round off the scene with a flourish.

The use of animal and sun imagery, as well as the reference to the myth of Phoebus, here accentuate the resumption of life in Claudio's departure for his new wedding ceremony.

ACT V · SCENE 4

Summary

All the major characters, except Don Pedro and Claudio, enter

Leonato's house. The friar is pleased that all has worked out well, as he knew it would. Leonato remarks that Don Pedro and Claudio are also innocent of any evil intent, and that they, like Margaret, were duped into participating in the plot. Benedick is also happy because he does not have to fight Claudio in a duel. Leonato reminds Antonio that he must pretend to be Hero's father and give her away to Claudio. Then Leonato sends the girls from the room and orders them to enter wearing masks when they are summoned. Benedick asks Leonato for permission to marry Beatrice. It is gladly given.

Don Pedro and Claudio arrive, attended by two or three others. Claudio says he is still willing to marry Leonato's niece and Antonio leaves to fetch her. There follows a witty exchange, in which it is shown that Benedick has a "February face,/So full of frost, of storm, and cloudiness." Apparently Benedick is frightened at the thought of getting married.

Antonio enters with all the girls, who are wearing masks. Antonio gives Hero to Claudio for his wife, but Leonato refuses to let the young count see his future wife's face until he has sworn to marry her. Claudio does so, and Hero takes off her mask. Don Pedro and Claudio are astounded, but the friar tells them he will explain everything after the marriage ceremony. Benedick and Beatrice engage in a short skirmish of wit that seems to show them both unable to declare love for each other. However, Claudio and Hero bring forth love sonnets that their friends have written about each other, and the marriage between Beatrice and Benedick is decided on. Benedick and Claudio are reconciled, and Benedick calls for music and dancing. Leonato, impatient to have the marriages performed, tells them there will be dancing afterward. But Benedick insists on dancing now and advises the Prince to find himself a wife. Typically, Benedick humorously reminds us of the theme of cuckolding: "There is no staff more reverend than one tipped with horn." (A married man is the most reverend or dignified.)

A messenger enters with the news that Don John has been captured and brought back under armed escort. Benedick says that he personally will devise "brave punishments" for him tomorrow, and orders the pipers to strike up the music.

Commentary

The purpose of this scene is to reconcile everyone, to remove all doubts, to bring the lovers together at last, and to present a celebration in honor of the coming marriages.

Assuming mastery for the first time in the play, Leonato calls the tune in this scene. Still impatient — he wishes to postpone the dance until *after* the wedding — he is his old practical and materialistic self, but agreeably so.

The Prince resumes his role as the witty, teasing lord and friend to the young grooms, Claudio and Benedick. His melancholy is a natural reaction to the marriages and the inevitable adjustments he will have to make.

Faithful to his promise to Leonato, Claudio is brave, even extreme, in taking a bride, sight unseen. There is an obsessive note in his carrying out the ritual penance and marrying Leonato's "niece." His witty baiting of Benedick is a more agreeable and endearing trait. Claudio leaves the audience with mixed feelings.

Benedick, the good-natured dupe, is still determined to go through with a wedding. He overcomes his natural timidity in order to get his way with Beatrice. Even at this late stage, he is still baffled by his friends' teasing about the way in which he was deceived into love. Like Benedick, Beatrice is the timid-but-determined wit going to her wedding.

Blank verse intensifies the emotions in the early part of this scene. First, Claudio and Hero must be reunited. Then, Benedick must persuade the Friar to marry a second set of lovers, and Benedick and Beatrice must undergo an appropriate amount of teasing.

The prose used in the remainder of the scene, as Benedick takes the lead, relaxes the tension. It is interrupted by a single blank-verse couplet, announcing that Don John, in custody, is being returned to Messina. Thus the emotions, after being heightened by the use of poetry in the early part of the scene, are relaxed through the use of prose at the end.

Structure

Methods of Analyzing Structure

The study of a Shakespearean play is never complete until the student has learned some of the means whereby Shakespeare has put the play together. The following methods of analyzing structure present some of the features prevalent in Shakespearean romantic comedy. The student should look for these features when analyzing other romantic comedies, and also attempt other methods of analysis.

1. Double Plot

It had become customary in Shakespeare's day to provide at least a double plot line in comedy. The inclusion of another plot line adds richness and a sense of completeness to the drama. The student will observe this more readily if he imagines how much would be lacking in *Much Ado* if the Beatrice-Benedick plot were excluded.

We see, therefore, that *Much Ado About Nothing* contains the tragicomic plot of Hero and Claudio, balanced by the comic story of Beatrice and Benedick. Usually, the secondary plot, in this case the story of Beatrice and Benedick, serves as a symbolic repetition of the themes and motifs found in the main plot line. In short, one mirrors the other in different terms. However, though this is true to a large extent in *Much Ado*, we note that the parallel development of both love stories stops at the church scene, in which Claudio denounces Hero (Act IV, Scene 1). From this point on, both plot lines go their different ways until the end of the play, when all delusion is cleared up and the characters are reunited in friendship and love.

2. Structural Levels

Elizabethan comedy generally includes a set of lower characters who provide comic relief and present the main story line in different terms through their bumbling behavior. *Much Ado About Nothing* contains two levels of development — one involving the main characters of noble or aristocratic background, and the other, the lower types who spring from common roots. Notice that Dogberry and his crew are not given a great amount of emphasis within the play. Their appearances are interspersed throughout the play to serve three functions: to create broad farcical humor; to provide the means of resolving the Don John-Hero-Claudio entanglement and to keep the tone of the play light; and to serve as a symbolic counterpart to the theme of pretence or affectation (notice how seriously they take their jobs and how important it is to Dogberry to present the appearance of formally dispatching his duties). Also observe that the two levels are developed only through Don Pedro, Claudio and Leonato on the upper level, and Dogberry and his crew on the lower level. Beatrice and

Benedick have nothing to do with the lower characters and their effect upon the development of the play.

3. Structural Outline

Shakespeare provides a clear line of development in his comedies. It is seldom difficult to examine his comedies, especially the different structural movements, without finding a very precise scheme for each major action. In short, a small amount of analysis will show us a clear skeletal outline of *Much Ado*. This, in turn, reveals the actual form the play has taken. For example, the first section of the play is actively concerned with setting up the Hero-Claudio marriage and some of the scheming of Don John. This development is concluded at the ball in Act II, Scene 1. This is the beginning. Beatrice and Benedick then take over, and their love story dominates the play until the church scene, in which Claudio denounces Hero. The play has now arrived at a drastic turning point, which ends the second section. This, therefore, constitutes the middle. The third section of the play, the end, is concentrated on solving the Hero-Claudio entanglement. Whereas the emphasis in the middle was upon Beatrice and Benedick, the end of the play once again returns to the Hero-Claudio plot and its influence upon the other characters. At the end of the play, all the different lines of development are unified. The student should attempt to trace the structural development of each set of characters. Once he has done this, it will become clear how artfully Shakespeare has intermingled the scenes to create a rich patchwork that in no way blurs any single structural line.

4. Analysis of Order

Notice that Shakespeare has consciously ordered the scenes to provide dramatic effect and meaning. Though Hero and Claudio would appear to be the main characters, Shakespeare has given a great deal of time and space to Beatrice and Benedick — practically the entire middle section of the play. Also, the structuring of Don John's scenes should leave no doubt that Shakespeare wanted us to concentrate primarily on the comedic aspects of the play, not the serious. After all, Don John is given only two short scenes alone with his servants in which to express his bitterness. He is shown telling lies in three additional scenes, but his dialogue is kept to a minimum. And he disappears completely in the last section of the play.

Questions and Answers on Structure

Question 1.

How does the play's structural development justify the emphasis on Beatrice and Benedick?

Answer

In Act II, Scene 1, we learn that Leonato has set Claudio's marriage day "a just sevennight" away. Don Pedro hits upon a scheme whereby everyone can spend the next week at the pleasurable task of making Beatrice and Benedick fall in love with each other. This serves, therefore, as the reason for the emphasis upon Beatrice and Benedick, and it also reminds us that a week is passing. Note that, after Don Pedro hits on his scheme, four of the following six scenes are devoted to Beatrice and Benedick. The order is: Act II, Scene 1 — the initiation of the scheme to bring them together; Act II, Scene 2 — Don John's and Borachio's scheme to thwart the marriage of Hero and Claudio; Act II, Scene 3 — the long scene in which Benedick is deceived into believing that Beatrice loves him; Act III, Scene 1 — a parallel to the preceding scene in that it shows Beatrice being deceived in the same manner that Benedick was; Act III, Scene 2 — the change in Benedick, who must now submit to merciless teasing about his being in love (note that the scene ends with a short bit of deception on the part of Don John); Act III, Scene 3 — the disclosure that Don John's plot has already been discovered; Act III, Scene 4 — a parallel to the teasing of Benedick when Hero and Margaret poke fun at Beatrice on the morning of the marriage. The end of the play satisfactorily blends the emphasis on Hero-Claudio and Beatrice-Benedick, the two couples finally being united in a double marriage. However, the justification of the four scenes of parallel growth is not merely that Beatrice and Benedick are entertaining. Observe that their story seems to restate and underscore the main issue of the play. Claudio is deceived and, as a result, figuratively falls out of love with Hero and loses her temporarily. Beatrice and Benedick are made to fall in love with each other by means of another deception and, ironically, seem to find happiness more readily than Hero and Claudio.

Question 2.

How do the lower characters fit in with the main plot line?

Answer

We must remember, first, that it was perfectly legitimate for the lower characters to bring about the means of a dramatic resolution in romantic comedy. Second, in case we should find it improbable that Dogberry would bring Leonato news of Conrade's and Borachio's capture, we should keep in mind that Dogberry is a police official. When he asks Leonato to examine the "two auspicious persons," he is dutifully reporting to his superior (the Governor of Messina). We also observe that the lower characters are tied to the main plot line, not only by their involvement with Leonato, but also because their actions display at least two symbolic parallels to the main action: 1) the device of eavesdropping is put to good use by the members of the watch when they purposely listen to Borachio explaining his villainy to Conrade; 2) the great emphasis that Dogberry and Verges place upon *charging* the watch, holding the examination, and conducting their affairs properly reminds us that they are as interested in outer appearances as Claudio and Don Pedro. We may also wonder why they delay so long in bringing Don John's villainy to light. We should keep in mind that Dogberry and his crew are not only incompetent, but also rather unsuccessful at making themselves understood by anyone outside of their own circle. It is for these reasons that Leonato loses his patience and does not allow Dogberry to name his prisoners or to state their villainy. We see, therefore, that the lower characters also serve as a modifying influence upon the serious tone of the play. If they are timely in nothing else, they at least show up soon enough to remind us that no matter how unpleasant things look, all will be made well very quickly.

Question 3.

Trace the main actions of the double plots in the three sections of the play, and show how they are related.

Answer

The double plots become clearer if we trace each one individually. The main action of the play, the Hero-Claudio story, is initiated and well advanced by the end of Act II, Scene 1. Claudio and Hero each take part in the deception of Beatrice and Benedick in the middle of the play, and little is heard concerning their marriage until Claudio leaves Hero at the altar in Act IV, Scene I. This marks the turning point in the main action, and leads to the false report of Hero's death, her subsequent disappearance, and the rift between Claudio and Benedick. The scene in which Benedick challenges Claudio is the same scene in which Claudio is informed of Don John's deception. This scene creates yet another deception and an additional turning point: Claudio swears to marry the niece of Leonato. (The effect of this new twist is somewhat weakened because we know that Leonato will substitute Hero for his supposed niece.) The marriage takes place and everyone is reconciled.

Beatrice and Benedick seem to assume importance almost from the very beginning of the play. After Claudio's marriage is arranged, Beatrice and Benedick take over for four out of the following six scenes. Hence, Beatrice and Benedick assume major proportions as Hero and Claudio drop into the background. The second part of the play, the middle, shows Beatrice and Benedick falling in love with each other and suffering the pangs of romantic love. Their story merges with the Hero-Claudio plot line at the end of the church scene in Act IV, Scene 1. From this point on, Beatrice and Benedick are opposed to

Claudio. This is the new direction they have taken after the turning point. Despite the fact that Benedick decides to challenge Claudio, Shakespeare does not allow Beatrice and Benedick to drop into the background of the Hero-Claudio story. The play's insistence on giving both couples an equal showing at the end demonstrates that Shakespeare considered the secondary story of Beatrice and Benedick as important as the conventional tragicomic love story of Hero and Claudio.

Question 4.

How does Shakespeare fit Don John into the structure of the play?

Answer

Shakespeare was faced with the problem of putting a villain into a comedy and at the same time maintaining a light tone. Shakespeare solves this problem in several ways: 1) Don John is presented as a conventional villain. He is a bastard and therefore his evil needs no explanation beyond his jealousy. Shakespeare devotes some time to the fact that Don Pedro is returning from an uprising Don John initiated. Hence, Don John's reputation precedes him. Furthermore, Don John is allowed to wonder aloud about his melancholy character — a symptom of a conventional sour personality — and other characters are required to discuss Don John in an unfavorable light. Therefore, we do not have to see much of Don John to believe him capable of mischief. 2) Shakespeare allows Don John to appear by himself (with his henchmen) only twice. These scenes are very short, and they show Don John *talking* about doing evil, not performing it. To make it appear that Don John's plotting is extremely distasteful, Shakespeare places these scenes almost immediately after the major events in the beginning of the play. For example, after Don Pedro promises to obtain Hero for Claudio, Shakespeare includes a very short scene between Leonato and Antonio. This scene reveals the first mistakenly overheard conversation. Don John appears in the next scene, learns the correct information and decides to wreck Claudio's happiness. The next scene takes place at the ball, during which Don Pedro successfully woos Hero for Claudio. In the scene that immediately follows, Act II, Scene 2, Don John decides to disgrace Hero. Therefore, though Don John is given little to do and say, his villainy appears every time a happy event occurs. This handling creates what one might call well-balanced villainy, if such a term can exist. 3) Don John is never allowed to monopolize a scene when he is performing his villainy. He appears at the very end of a scene or for a short space in "French scenes" (scenes in which a character, or characters, enter or leave.) When Don John tells Claudio that the Prince loves Hero, Claudio is alone, and Don John is permitted to speak only a few lines. Don John is again shown in action in Act III, Scene 2, but he is not on stage more than five minutes of this very long scene. Of course, in this scene he discredits Hero, but only after great sport has been made of Benedick's love-sickness. And finally, in Act IV, Scene 1, Don John contributes only nine lines to the denunciation of Hero (notice that Don John allows Claudio to do most of the accusing). The actual deception, which Don John arranged, is only described. 4) As we pointed out before, Dogberry and the members of the watch discover Don John's evil deception not more than a half-hour after it has been committed. Of course, this undercuts the effectiveness of the deception. And again, Dogberry shows up at various times to remind us, as soon as he can get to the point, that good will prevail and that we ought not to fear for the happiness of the main characters. 5) Don John is removed from the play at the turning point and is not seen again. He ceases to be a threatening force. Shakespeare could have brought him back at the end, in chains, for example, but this would have ruined the gay mood. It is more effective to keep him offstage and let us imagine him as the foiled villain.

Characters

Methods of Analyzing Characters

1. Character Description

It is useful for the student to prepare a short summation of each character. The summation should contain the major actions of each character as well as a brief account of the character's own reasons for his behavior. A similar account of the character's physical attributes and some of the remarks other characters make about him will fill out the picture quite amply. (For example, Hero is described as being short and Claudio is referred to as a very young man. Hero, of course, cannot act "small" or "short," but we do see from Claudio's actions that he frequently behaves like a little boy. Hence, we get the picture of two doll-like characters, one a petite little girl and the other a baby-faced young man.) It will also be useful if the student adds to the summary a few words showing a contrast between each character and some of the other characters, especially with another character that seems to parallel (in this sense, Benedick would be parallel to Claudio).

2. Character Analysis

After summations of the characters have been made, the student should proceed to analyze the characters in depth. A standard rule to remember is that a character's major actions and decisions determine his reason for being in the play. These actions project the character's individual *reactions* to a situation. A character's lesser actions or philosophy — brought out in his dialogue — not only add rich variety to the profile of the individual, but supply consistently logical character development. The major action of each character must be in keeping with his past behavior or we have a feeling of disbelief. This is what is meant when we say an action is "in character" or "out of character." Finally, after we have listed the major and minor actions and decisions, the philosophy of the character, the quirks, outlook, personality traits, and the logic in the growth of a character, we may contrast the character by placing him in the situations of other characters in the play. Two cases in point would be: 1) we observe that Benedick's outlook on life is rather realistic. Were he in Claudio's position, he certainly would not have acted as Claudio does. Had Benedick been deceived about Hero, his actions would not have been so extreme. He probably would have thanked his stars he was no longer linked to one so young and unfaithful, denied any further responsibility for her and considered the matter closed. Of course, he would have been hurt, but there is reason to believe he also would have "chalked it up to experience." 2) Beatrice is shown, in word and deed, as an articulate young girl who believes in women's rights, at least to a degree greater than Leonato allows Hero. Had Beatrice been accused, we may be certain she would not have been struck dumb, as Hero was. Rather than faint, she would have fought back. The upshot would have been that her accusers would have left the church, ashamed and degraded by her agile defence and sharp wit.

3. Character Recognition

Often Shakespeare created characters, or groups of characters, that develop in a parallel fashion. Also, Shakespeare included "types" or "conventional" characters. However, his handling of these types is never a stereotyped treatment.

Parallel Characters

Parallel characters in Shakespeare's plays often define each other by their opposing outlook on life or their differing behavior patterns. It is clear that the Hero-Claudio tragicomedy is meant to parallel the Beatrice-Benedick comic love story. Yet, if we look at each of the characters separately, the character of Benedick, for example, helps define that of Claudio. The opposite is also true. The same may be said of Beatrice and Hero, though Hero's shyness helps to clarify Beatrice more than our articulate heroine can possibly define the conventional Hero. Further parallelism is observed when we note that Hero and Claudio are attracted to each other because they are very much alike. The same holds true for Beatrice and Benedick. However, the student should be careful not to place too much emphasis upon two parallel groups of characters. The deepest meaning we find in character comes from the differences between the parallel characters as individuals. Their decisions, and their actions — especially in the case of *Much Ado* — alienate them at first and finally bring them back together.

Conventional Characters

Conventional characters also go under the title of "stock" characters — that is, characters who stand for a certain outlook or behavior pattern which has become accepted or expected. The student will benefit by learning to recognize these characters. Hero and Claudio represent certain conventional features of the romantic courtly world view that had become prevalent in literature during Shakespeare's time. Leonato and Antonio also represent certain set characters who appear in romantic comedy as the paternal or family influence exerted over other characters. A character such as the friar is indispensable to a tragicomedy, since his behavior, or rather, his reasoning power, serves usually as the resolving factor in the dilemma. Of course, there is Don John whose villainy was probably laughed at by the audience since he stood for the most extreme kind of behavior in a current theory of "humors."

4. Lower Characters

Shakespeare's comedies also have a set of lower characters. These characters provide humor and, though they most often are not richly characterized, they are indeed very endearing. Note that the lower characters in the plays are really Englishmen, even when they are supposed to be dwelling in another country. Their speech is that of English commoners and, though we may feel Shakespeare's keen satirical wit as he puts these characters through their paces, we are also touched by the humanity and love with which he draws them. The lower characters are often tied to the main, or upper, story line, because they are minor officials, or are related to or are servants of some of the major characters. Much confusion is removed when we observe that the lower characters' actions serve as reflections of the major plot lines. This, of course, is a strengthening factor in the drama because it creates a repetition of the story lines in the mind of the spectator.

Finally, the student should remember that the lower characters are frequently motivated by a single driving force that far exceeds their other personality traits. We have seen this in Dogberry's concern with formality and the subsequent use of malapropisms it creates. The lower characters in Shakespeare's comedies are a little world unto themselves. The student will greatly benefit from placing them in clear perspective within the play.

Character Sketches

Hero

She is the shy, modest daughter of Leonato and the fiancée of Claudio. She is also a conventional, well-bred young lady of high position. She has learned to obey her father in all things and to remain silent in the company of gentlemen. She is, of course, the opposite of Beatrice. Her behavior is demure, though she gaily participates in deceiving Beatrice. Her major lines are spoken in poetry, imparting a romantic aura to her story. One of Hero's serious limitations as a character is her inability to speak up. This is shown most clearly when she is accused of being unfaithful to Claudio. However, we may assume correctly that the harsh accusation frightens and shames her into silence, though she has nothing to be ashamed of. She faints when Claudio breaks into tears and swears he will never love again. Of course, her innocent character and sweet personality are noted by the friar. At the suggestion of the friar, Hero's death is reported, and she goes into seclusion until Don John's plot is revealed. At the end of the play, she is reunited with Claudio.

Claudio

He is the male counterpart of Hero. He is a young nobleman who has proved his bravery in battle. Perhaps his upbringing is a little too "proper," since we feel his love for Hero is secondary to the very practical and brilliant match he wishes to arrange for himself. He is quick to become jealous and even quicker to believe the very worst about the woman he loves. However, these peculiar traits are partially explained by his extreme naïveté. He is also quick to enter into a playful plot by which he hopes to cause Benedick and Beatrice to fall in love. He tolerates Benedick's jesting with good humor, and returns it when the occasion permits. He is genuinely repentant when he learns the truth about Hero, but his promise to marry Leonato's niece, sight unseen, is a display of submissiveness, as well as a genuine act of self-denial. At the end of the play, he is brought back to the world of reality when he learns that Hero is not dead.

Beatrice

She can be described as quick-witted, articulate, wise, faithful, vivacious, wilful and charming, along with many other sparkling adjectives. She teases Hero about letting Leonato, Beatrice's uncle, choose a husband for her. Beatrice advises Hero to make sure her husband is handsome, an indication that Beatrice has given the subject of marriage some thought. She jokes unceasingly about the bothersome state of marriage, yet she is clever enough to know a church when she sees one. She can tease Benedick out of all patience, but she also surrenders her love immediately when she is certain he is telling the truth about his love for her. She is wise enough to know that courtship and marriage can be the cause of repenting if one does not act wisely. She realizes that Benedick will be proud of her and will not limit her freedom. Her faithfulness to her cousin is touching. She never wavers from it, even at the risk of losing Benedick. When she overhears her faults being discussed she immediately submits to better judgment in order to mend them. At the end of the play, when she learns she has been tricked, she pretends to be annoyed. In reality she wants just a word or two more to convince her of Benedick's sincerity.

Benedick

Like Claudio, Benedick is a brave soldier, a nobleman and a gentleman. However, unlike Claudio, Benedick gives the impression of maturity. He is a confirmed bachelor and swears he will never fall in love. But when he learns that Beatrice loves him, his defences crumble. He falls "horribly" in love with her, and even assumes the role of the courtly lover. He soon gives up this pretence, however, for he realizes he cannot woo in "festival" terms. Benedick is as articulate as Beatrice, but when overcome by the new and strange emotions of love, he turns to speaking paradoxically. He has a strong sense of justice. It is this feeling for right and his love for Beatrice that prompt him to challenge Claudio. Yet he is delighted when he learns that the duel need not take place. His final submission to love — that is, marrying Beatrice at the end of the play — parallels Beatrice's own reversal of avowed spinsterhood.

Leonato

Hero's father and Beatrice's uncle is the elderly Governor of Messina. He typifies somewhat the conventional old man, or elderly parent, found in tragicomedies. Shakespeare satirizes Leonato's conventionality by showing him more interested in securing a highly respectable marriage for his daughter than in allowing her to express her own feelings. After Claudio's angry departure, Leonato's rather stereotyped fury aimed at Hero is partially offset by the friar's reasoning. When Leonato later encounters Claudio and Don Pedro, he is angrier at their having spoiled his good name than at Hero's defamation. His revenge upon Claudio provides another little game of deception.

Antonio

Leonato's brother has very little to do in the play. He rages at Don Pedro and Claudio soon after advising his brother to remain moderate. His main function in the play is to pretend to give away his "daughter" — Hero — to Claudio, who thinks she is Leonato's niece.

Don John

He is, of course, the villain of the play. He is melancholy, evil by nature, and contemptuous of love or human feelings. He is outspoken about his villainy and hides his spitefulness under the guise of plain-dealing. He tells us more about his evil than he shows us. However, we learn that he is envious of Claudio's rise to fame at his expense, and that he will go to any lengths to destroy the marriage of the young "start-up". His evil plot fails, and he is apprehended soon after his departure from Messina.

Don Pedro

The Prince of Arragon is a good-natured, fun-loving nobleman. He genuinely enjoys the company of his friends and is quick to participate in any event that will create good sport and merriment. He readily agrees to woo Hero for Claudio because he is anxious to help out his timid friend, and because it is an amusing little game for him. He devises the brilliant idea of trying to cause Beatrice and Benedick to fall in love by means of a deception. He, like Claudio, is guilty of accepting appearance for reality when he agrees with Claudio's unwarranted accusation of Hero's unfaithfulness. Don Pedro should have looked further into the situation. In any case, we do not feel there is any evil intent in his conduct. At the end of the play, the truth is revealed to him and he learns, like Claudio, the danger of arriving at premature conclusions about other people.

Borachio and Conrade

They are convincing villains. Borachio willingly performs an evil act for Don John and boasts about it in the streets. This leads to his arrest and the subsequent revelation of Don John's plot against Hero and Claudio. Conrade is not as evil as his friend, but he too swears to help carry out Don John's plot. Shakespeare uses Conrade and Borachio primarily to initiate the main conflict of the play.

Dogberry, Verges and Members of the Watch

These are the policemen in the play. However, Dogberry's and Verges' bumbling efforts to bring the culprits to justice are indeed not meant to symbolize any higher meaning. Their stupidity and talkativeness provide a satirical view of certain lower-class officials. One hardly knows how they do it, but they succeed in capturing the slanderers, bringing them to justice and resolving the major conflict of the play.

Friar Francis

A reasonable, calm, and intelligent man, he is also a good judge of character. He discovers a way of freeing Hero from the stigma Don Pedro and Claudio have put on her character, thus providing the structural motivation for the outcome of the play. Beyond this, he has little else to do. The friar's long speeches in Act IV, Scene 1, contain some of the most beautiful poetry in the play.

Minor Characters

The SEXTON appears very briefly to write down the confession of Borachio; the MESSENGER brings us news of Don Pedro's victory in the beginning of the play; BALTHASAR, a servant of Don Pedro, provides the singing; URSULA, one of Hero's gentlewomen, co-operates in the deception of Beatrice; MARGARET, another gentlewoman, unwittingly aids Borachio in Don John's plot against her mistress.

Questions and Answers on Characters
Question 5.

How is Claudio given the characteristics of a little boy, and in what ways is he a rather conventional character?

Answer

Claudio is extremely naïve. It is true that he may have liked Hero before he went to war, but now that he has returned, she has caught his fancy even more than before. He immediately allows himself to fall in love without any further consideration. When Don John tells Claudio that Don Pedro loves Hero and plans to marry her, Claudio believes him (Act II, Scene 1). Later, after Don Pedro explains the mistake, Claudio becomes impatient and decides to get married immediately: "Tomorrow, my lord. Time goes on crutches till Love have all his rites." Another aspect of his naïveté is apparent in Act III, Scene 2. The day before the marriage Claudio offers to interrupt his honeymoon and accompany Don Pedro back to Arragon. Claudio's eagerness to believe the worst, or to perform a self-sacrificing, ingratiating act, prepares us for his later abuse of Hero. In Act II, Scene 3, Claudio believes Don John's slur on Hero's reputation before it has been proved. The slightest hint of her unfaithfulness is enough to wound his vanity, to make him think he has been rejected, and to give him the motivation to strike back through an extravagant plan of revenge. At the wedding, though we may feel his hurt is real, his berating of Hero and his childish crying imply wilfulness more than sensitivity.

Evidence of Claudio's being conventional appears in Act I, Scene 1, when he asks Don Pedro if Leonato has a son. Of course, Claudio is performing the very task which his father taught him — that is, marry *well*! Give love its due *after* the dowry has been delivered. In true courtly form, Claudio allows Don Pedro to settle the marriage bargain for him, and when Claudio thinks that Don Pedro has betrayed him, his silent jealousy and suffering are signs of the courtly idea of manliness. After the marriage has been arranged, Claudio's preoccupation turns to love songs, ballads and courtly wooing of his lady love. Not only is Claudio's plan of revenge an elaborately childish contrivance, but it is suitable in the extreme to the courtly code that rules the wounded vanity of noblemen. His encounter with Leonato and Antonio shows his courtly respect for old men, yet we still feel that he loves to act like a brave soldier and to prove how valiant he is in battle. The punishment he inflicts upon himself is proportionately as extreme as his revenge upon Hero. His morality is a conventional, puritanical morality: sin is sin; retribution is swift, merciless and unremitting. His very conventionality *requires* that he punish himself in a manner suitable to the elaborateness of his guilt. This, of course, reflects the romantic, courtly tradition of virtue and righteousness.

Question 6.
Explain the influence of Don John's character in the play.

Answer
Don John, the illegitimate brother of Don Pedro, is also a rather conventional character. His conventionality lies in his being illegitimate, his pure evil, the hatred he has for his legitimate brother and Claudio (whose star rose at his expense), and his sour outlook on the world in general. All this needs no motivation since Don John, as a villainous character, was expected to behave in this manner. Yet, Don John is not only a melancholy villain. He is a liar and a vile slanderer, as well as an outrageous coward, preferring to scheme in secret and to discredit rather than face an opponent directly. Though lying and slandering are extremely loathsome, Shakespeare never allows Don John to pose a definite threat. (Remember that Dogberry discovers the plot very early.) What is interesting about Don John is that his character acts as a catalyst on the other characters. He provides the major complication in the play and the situations that allow the other characters to reveal themselves through their behavior. Don John is a conventional villain, but Shakespeare's treatment goes beyond the conventional and on to the satirical because of Don John's singularly evil approach to everything.

Question 7.

Discuss the similarities in the characters of Beatrice and Benedick.

Answer

Shakespeare purposely drew Beatrice and Benedick so that they would define each other through similarities. Throughout the play, each of them is searching and questioning. They have seen through the artificial conduct of contemporary "high fashion" and have little more than contempt for the falseness of society.

Both are rather frightened of marriage — Beatrice fears losing her individuality and Benedick's humorous jests about cuckolding suggest a fear of losing his manhood. Yet we feel that they are really interested in getting married, since it is usual to avoid a subject one dislikes, rather than talk it to death. This is true also in the assumed hostility of the "merry war" these characters engage in.

Beatrice supposedly does not like Benedick. Is this why her first words are about his safety? She thinks he is conceited, yet she cannot stop talking about him. Benedick thinks of Beatrice as "Lady Disdain" herself, yet he, too, finds her so fascinating that his conversation constantly refers to the emotions she creates in him.

Both are able to learn about their faults and set about mending them. Their humanity is more important to them than the reputation of being a cold-hearted maiden would be to Beatrice or that of being a contemptuous lover would be to Benedick.

Each is willing to undergo the trials of love to learn. Hence, Beatrice and Benedick subject themselves to the pains of love. The scene in the church snaps them out of their affected appearance of love, especially since they have seen Claudio laboring under a delusion that Hero appears to be guilty of infidelity.

Finally, each is able to stand outside of the situation and call upon reason in place of emotion. They alone have enough presence of mind either to take care of Hero, who has fainted (Beatrice), or to remain silent and not get involved in the high pitch of emotional intensity (Benedick). The Hero-Claudio situation, of course, is what eventually brings Beatrice and Benedick together.

Question 8.

Show how Dogberry is raised above the level of an ordinary clown.

Answer

Dogberry is given a very active part in the play. He is allowed to control the resolving factor — that is, the revelation that Borachio has confessed Don John's evil slander and deception. Symbolically, Dogberry's preoccupation with maintaining the exact formality of his position is comparable to the affected roles some of the other characters play — Claudio, for example, whose life is ruled by the conventions of the courtly romantic, and Leonato, whose fear of slander is more important at first than his daughter's innocence or feelings. Dogberry's malapropisms are at times only the results of his attempting to speak in a manner exceeding, not only his education, but also his station in life. His examination (Act IV, Scene 2) of the two villains, Conrade and Borachio, redefines the lamentation over Hero in the preceding scene. His slowness in bringing the crime to light serves to tone down the evil of Don John, as well as to provide a little suspense.

Meaning

Methods of Analyzing Meaning

1. Thematic Analysis

The theme of a play is the abstract meaning, or the main idea, which the events of the play illustrate. A play may sometimes have a major theme and a secondary theme, or themes. We learn to recognize a theme by analyzing the imagery, symbolism, actions and devices in the play. Our analysis, therefore, is concerned with the direction in which these various elements of drama are pointing and what they demonstrate to us. In a well-written play, all the elements of drama serve to support the major theme.

2. Emphasis

In analyzing the meaning of a play, we may generally assume that a playwright always has control of his material. We note, then, that the various movements of a play, the amount of time devoted to a particular character or action, the length of a scene, and the strength of its language are all controlled, more or less, by the emphasis the playwright has placed on them. Our task is to determine the amount of emphasis placed on particular aspects of the drama, and to derive understanding from the author's intent.

3. Symbolic Values

A symbol is something that stands for something else (the student has probably learned long ago that a verbal definition of "symbol" is hard to come by). A symbol may be a physical object, or it may be an image or a concept. In any case, the meaning of a symbol is expanded beyond its immediate association. Symbols take on abstract values that have a direct bearing upon the theme. In fact, symbols often *create* much of the content of a theme. Learning to recognize symbols and their application to the theme of the play will help to clarify the meaning of a drama.

4. Application of the Theme

We have not fully grasped the meaning of a play until we are able to apply its theme to our own lives, or to the broad field of human relationships. Is the theme of the play didactic (does it teach us something), or does it present a practical approach to living, therefore making it utilitarian? Perhaps it presents a moral code we ought to observe in order to maintain peace and security in society. We must determine how it applies to mankind.

Comedies, like serious plays, can be categorized. Recognizing the type of comedy we have observed will probably aid us in an application of the theme. Farce is a form of comedy that is thinly constructed, and though it does not contain the rich elements of a higher form, it can provide an evening of good fun. A comedy of manners, sophisticated, snobbish in its outlook, yet witty, can make a number of pertinent remarks about society and the ways that people relate to each other. However, a higher form of comedy is the universal comedy, the kind of intellectual exhibition that seldom makes us laugh heartily. This type of comedy views man's existence in the light of reason. In this kind of play, it is the difference between what man *does* and what he *ought* to do in the light of reason, not emotion, that provides the comedy. This form of comedy is filled with something more meaningful than loud laughter, and that is the *spirit* of comedy. It is from this kind of comedy that we receive universal truths which can be applied to man's life. Where does *Much Ado About Nothing* belong in the scale of comedy? Once the student has determined the play's comedy range, the application of the theme should become evident.

Questions and Answers on Meaning

Question 9.

What is the theme of *Much Ado About Nothing*?

Answer

Much Ado About Nothing has a number of themes. However, the main theme seems to be concerned with appearance versus reality, or truth as opposed to falsehood. One arrives at this conclusion because the device of eavesdropping is used throughout the play for all three levels of action — the Hero-Claudio tragicomedy, the Beatrice-Benedick love story, and the tribulations of Dogberry and his crew. Most of the overheard discussions are really deceptions. The eavesdroppers in these cases really believe what they are seeing or hearing is true. Even the main action of the play is based on a deception. Furthermore, the means of resolving the dilemma caused by Don John's villainous plot is brought about by another overheard conversation, and the final portion of the play is devoted to yet an additional major deception (the "death" of Hero and Claudio's belief he is marrying Leonato's niece). We see, therefore, that some of the characters in the play are quick to seize upon half-truths and to allow themselves to be misled as a result. The outcome almost borders on the tragic.

Parallel to this major theme is the theme of moderation. This secondary theme is derived from the actions of Beatrice and Benedick who, unlike Claudio, Leonato, Don Pedro, and Antonio, desire to change their sense of values and amend their faults. Beatrice and Benedick quickly fall in love with each other. After a short period of acting out the conventional behavior expected of lovers — affectations in dress, manners and speech, as well as love-sickness, jealousy and pettiness — they decide to abandon all pretence and act in a normal fashion. It seems, therefore, that human feelings expressed through moderate, reasonable channels of behavior are more natural and meaningful. This is especially true if we contrast the behavior patterns of Beatrice and Benedick with those of Claudio. Claudio's code of honor is extreme. His rashness results in near tragedy, whereas Beatrice and Benedick, through their acceptance of moderation, find a path to happiness much sooner than Claudio does.

Question 10.

How does the emphasis upon conventionality fit into the play's meaning?

Answer

Those characters in the play that are conventional types either suffer terrible reversals or are completely frustrated in their designs. For example, Hero, Claudio, Leonato, Don Pedro, and Don John are each presented as conventional characters belonging to the circle of courtly life or romantic tradition. Hero typifies the obedient daughter, Claudio the courtly lover, Don Pedro the dignified, kindly prince, and Leonato the elderly father. Claudio's exaggerated sense of honor leads him to discredit Hero without really acquiring adequate proof. Hero is conventionally shy and demure, so much so that she does not even speak up in her own defence. Leonato, obeying the rules for fathers whose daughters have abused the family name, calls down the wrath of heaven upon his child.

Don John also fits into the conventional mold, but in his particular case, we see that Shakespeare is satirizing the stereotyped villain. The first four characters are almost ruined by the effects of their conventional behavior. However, Don John is completely thwarted in every evil scheme he undertakes. This is not to say that Shakespeare is undercutting all that is accepted as normal in aristocratic society. But Shakespeare is undercutting the *pretentious* norms of behavior that society (the upper-class society or court tradition) sanctions. Hence, Shakespeare is showing the reverse of society's stereotyped view, especially aristocratic or romantic morality, and showing that the warmth of sincere human relationships is far preferable to insincere affectation.

Question 11.

How does the imagery of war or battle reflect upon the theme?

Answer

Much of the theme of this play is concerned with conventional behavior. Hence, we find Claudio at the beginning returning victoriously from the wars. He finds a beautiful young girl and desires to marry her. This is in keeping with the romantic tradition, since only the brave deserve the fair. However, warfare is not dropped after Claudio's initial entrance. It is carried further into the play as we witness the "merry war" and "skirmishes of wit" between Beatrice and Benedick. In fact, warfare takes on a figurative meaning when we later see that it has come to involve Hero and Claudio as opponents.

The literary and courtly tradition considered love-making a kind of combat between the lover and the lady. The lover tries to attain his desires by every means his wit can devise. The lady, however, remains aloof, giving battle frequently and remaining indifferent to the onslaughts of the sighing lover. There is a suggestion of this in the later difficulties between Hero and Claudio, and a stronger inference of it in Beatrice's and Benedick's romance. In this manner, the conventional romantic tradition of a figurative battle between the lover and his lady is subtly carried through the play by means of suggestion, rather than direct statement.

Question 12.

State the major images of the play and show their relationship to the themes.

Answer

WAR AND BATTLE: As has just been discussed, the images of war and battle point out the conventional love duel that was considered a traditional part of the trials of a young man and his lady love.

CUCKOLDING: This particular image, though foreign to modern understanding, underscores Benedick's unswerving denial of women and marriage. This denial might be considered a conventional behavior pattern of confirmed bachelors, but the image and its reference are used mostly in jest. It is soon put aside as Benedick becomes more susceptible to the charms of Beatrice. In short, this distrust of women begins to vanish as he becomes more aware of the warmth of genuine love.

Style

Methods of Analyzing Style

A playwright's style is the manner in which his play is expressed verbally. However, style is also considered the unique way in which the playwright approaches his subject and handles it. Hence, we see that a playwright's style is both verbal and intellectual, and constitutes the complete expression of his dramatic artistry.

1. Diction

Diction consists of the playwright's use of particular words in a particular order. If the student will observe the diction in *Much Ado About Nothing*, or in any play for that matter, he will notice that "figurative language" — simile, metaphor, personification, antithesis, hyperbole, to name a few types — is employed extensively. Figurative expressions give color and variety to the dialogue of the play. Without figurative expression, the language in a play would be flat and undramatic. The student should always be aware that the language spoken in a play is not necessarily the same kind of language we speak in everyday life. A dramatic composition is a work of art. Its language, therefore, is heightened, even though it may be meant to resemble normal speech. Also, a play is perhaps the most economical of the art forms. Its language is condensed in comparison to a novel. Therefore, we see that a play's language must be intense, full and rich, yet concise enough to fit into two and a half, or three hours, of time.

2. Imagery

Imagery is the conscious or unconscious pictures or associations we get when we read a work of literature or see a play. In a play, images are suggested by the language and figures of speech the characters employ. This is not to say that Shakespeare consciously strove to include particular images in his play in an exacting fashion. Though this *may* be the case, it is also possible that certain feelings or moods were pressing upon Shakespeare's consciousness as he wrote *Much Ado About Nothing*. As a result, these feelings or moods are expressed more or less consistently throughout the play. Imagery also helps to define the play in figurative terms. In *Much Ado* the images of cuckolding, masks, battle, and dancing, to mention a few, appear in varying intensity. It is useful to isolate the various images in a play by analyzing their relevancy, frequency, and intensity. In this manner we are able to define the play in terms of figurative symbols.

3. Language Levels

Often plays contain a number of different levels of language.

Various characters from different environments speak in different ways. The language they employ helps define them as characters and sheds light on their backgrounds and environment. A playwright's style is observed in his use of different levels of language and the skill with which he carries out this most difficult task. Shakespeare is noted for including many language levels in his plays. *Much Ado* is a fine example. The play contains three different levels of expression: prose, constituting the major portion of the play's language; verse, used primarily in relation to the Hero-Claudio tragicomedy; and the language of the lower characters. In each case, the language employed serves as a means of defining the character of individuals or groups.

4. Point of View

A strong feature of a playwright's style is his point of view: his approach to his material and the manner in which he handles his subject matter. Playwrights such as Euripides, Shakespeare, Ibsen, and George Bernard Shaw are noted for writing more than pretty little plays that follow all the rules. Their intellectual approach to their subjects is to use conventional material in a way that points out the falseness, stupidity, superstition or injustice of society's morality and inflexible regulations. *Much Ado* is a good case in point. Shakespeare assembles a group of conventional characters and allows them to run up and down the scale of their emotions (hence the tone of tragicomedy). So ridiculous is their exaggerated behavior, that we begin to see it in the light of social satire. Shakespeare is mocking society's accepted conventional morality.

Questions and Answers on Style

Question 13.
Discuss the significance of the use of prose in the play.

Answer
There are three levels of language in *Much Ado About Nothing*: 1) prose, spoken by everyone; 2) verse, devoted primarily to the tragicomic elements of the play; 3) the language of the lower characters, spoken by Dogberry and his crew. Prose, being the vehicle for comedy, is used the most extensively in the Beatrice-Benedick comic plot. Prose is very flexible and allows a speaker to pause without ruining the meter, or to play with the words. Furthermore, prose enables the characters to make witty remarks and continue them throughout an entire scene. In the case of the Beatrice-Benedick love story, prose is necessary because verse would dilute the comedy, as well as create a confusion of tones. Also, prose sets up the theatrical convention of realism. In *Much Ado* this is important because Beatrice and Benedick are given the attributes of realistic-minded people whose

thought and language set them apart from the more stereotyped characters who speak in verse. Notice that Beatrice and Benedick hardly ever speak in blank verse. In Act IV, Scene 1, Beatrice and Benedick each have a few lines of verse. In Act V, Scene 4, they once again speak a few lines in verse. In the first instance cited, the verse is used for contrast — Beatrice's ten lines contrast nicely with the parallel prose speech of Benedick in Act II, Scene 3. The other two snatches of verse spoken by Beatrice and Benedick are included in the play because both scenes (the denunciation in the church and the reunion at the end) maintain a poetic tone. Yet Beatrice and Benedick do not wait long before switching back to their true form of expression.

In passing, it is interesting to note Hardin Craig's tally of prose and verse lines in the play: there are 2,826 lines of dialogue in the play, 2,106 of them in prose and only 643 in blank verse.

Question 14.

Discuss at least three features of the play that reveal Shakespeare's point of view.

Answer

Shakespeare approaches his material with the idea of undercutting (that is, making trivial) the major characters and their actions in the play. (He uses the same approach in *Troilus and Cressida*, in which he deflates the reputation of the Greek legendary heroes.) In *Much Ado*, Shakespeare wishes to show the emptiness of courtly morality and the artificial humanity it imposes upon its followers. First, therefore, we find Claudio depicted as a very conventional young man who requires economic advancement as a pre-requisite to his getting married. Hero is also shown as the conventionally obedient daughter of a high-ranking public official. Beside them is Don John whose paper-tiger villainy is foiled by a group of bumbling oafs. Contrasted to this set of characters are Beatrice and Benedick, who lay firm hold upon the *realities* of life.

Second, Shakespeare takes great care to provide plenty of melodrama in the very scenes in which the conventional characters are supposed to be in dead earnest. This occurs especially in Act IV, Scene 1, when Claudio denounces Hero and leaves in tears after Hero faints. Leonato quickly follows up Claudio's rash behavior by his unfatherly attitude toward his own daughter. This is followed in Act V, Scene 1 by an outrageous scene of blustering and ranting by Leonato and Antonio. Shakespeare purposely creates the picture of two older men insulting Don Pedro and Claudio and challenging them to duels. The scene is made not only melodramatic by the bluster, but laughable when we remember that Hero is not dead and Leonato is mostly angry because of the slur Don Pedro and Claudio have put upon his family name.

A third feature of the point of view is the almost mock-heroic treatment given to the dramatic high points of the play. A pattern is formed which shows Shakespeare's satire. After Claudio has denounced Hero, he cannot leave the poor girl in peace until he has uttered the final statement demanded of the brokenhearted lover by convention:

> O Hero! what a Hero hadst thou been
> If half thy outward graces had been placed
> About thy thoughts and counsels of thy heart!
> But fare thee well, most foul, most fair, Farewell,
> Thou pure impiety and impious purity!
> For thee I'll lock up all the gates of love,
> And on my eyelids shall conjecture hang,
> To turn all beauty into thoughts of harm,
> And never shall it more be gracious.

Notice the whining tone of the first three lines and the affected accounting of Hero in terms of opposites in the fourth and fifth lines. The last four lines are devoted to Claudio himself and how terrible his suffering will be. It is indeed a bright young man who can spout well-turned phrases at such a crucial moment. Or perhaps they were very adequately rehearsed the night before in order to keep his diction well in keeping with the elaborateness of the denunciation! In Act V, Scene 1, Antonio and Leonato encounter Don Pedro and Claudio. Just a few minutes previously, Antonio had counselled Leonato to remain calm. The brothers both decide that a demonstration of pure anger will not succeed and that they must use reason to get even with their enemies (of course the *enemies* are the slanderers of Leonato's good name — Don Pedro and Claudio). The scene becomes funny, as well as ironically ridiculous when Leonato is forced to hold his brother in check. Antonio is reduced to the level of name-calling:

> **Leonato:** Brother —
>
> **Antonio:** Content yourself. God knows I loved my niece,
> And she is dead, slandered to death by villains,
> That dare as well answer a man indeed
> As I dare take serpent by the tongue.
> Boys, apes, braggarts, Jacks, milksops!
>
> **Leonato:** Brother Anthony —
>
> **Antonio:** Hold you content. What, man! I know them, yea,
> And what they weigh, even to the utmost scruple,
> Scrambling, outfacing, fashion-monging boys,
> That lie and cog and flout, deprave and slander,
> Go anticly, show outward hideousness,

And speak off half a dozen dang'rous words,
How they might hurt their enemies, if they durst;
And this is all.

Leonato: But, brother Antony —

Antonio: Come, 'tis no matter.
Do not you meddle; let me deal in this.

All this from the wise, patient elders of the community! Claudio's visit to Hero's family monument is, in itself, a comical mock-heroic effort at reproducing a genuine elegy or lament. The deflation is complete when Claudio states: "Now unto thy bones good night!/Yearly will I do this rite." And finally, a short interchange at the end of the play caps the entire proceedings:

> **Claudio:** Give me your hand, before this holy friar.
> I am your husband if you like of me.
>
> **Hero:** And when I lived I was your other wife; [unmasks]
> And when you loved you were my other husband.
>
> **Claudio:** Another Hero!
>
> **Hero:** Nothing certainer.
> One Hero died defiled; but I do live,
> And surely as I live, I am a maid.
>
> **Don Pedro:** The former Hero! Hero that is dead!
>
> **Leonato:** She died, my lord, but whiles her slander lived.

All the intrigue that surrounded the marriage has been put to rest in nine or ten lines that incredibly enough resolve the play without any questioning from Claudio or Don Pedro. In fairness, it should be stated that the friar says he will explain everything *after* the wedding. The naïve innocence of the characters as they engage in such a momentous event is the final touch of satire which Shakespeare employs.

Question 15.

Trace the imagery of war or battle in the play. Explain its significance.

Answer

The opening lines of the play announce the outcome of a war, and we are then told that Claudio performed the "feats of a lion" in battle. Beatrice's first remark is a jesting inquiry about Benedick: "I pray you, is Signior Mountanto returned from the wars or no?" (Mountanto was a term for a fencing thrust.) Beatrice continues talking about Benedick in terms of a verbal battle, in which he engaged with her when he first arrived in Messina. Leonato then states the reason for

Beatrice's remarks about Benedick when he tells us of their "merry war." Whenever they meet "there's a skirmish of wit between them." The imagery, which has been provided from the very beginning, gives us a suggestion of the relationship between Beatrice and Benedick. Of course this relationship is brought into clear focus when Benedick arrives and a "skirmish of wit" ensues. From then on, a good portion of the play is devoted to Beatrice and Benedick, the playful war between them and the efforts on the part of their friends to bring about a truce. There are additional suggestive images of fencing or duelling which refer indirectly to war, especially when Antonio, Leonato and Benedick challenge Claudio at different times within the same scene. Benedick is not in a mood for jesting, and he says to Claudio:

> Sir, I shall meet your wit in the career and you charge it against me. I pray you choose another subject. ["Career" means headfirst.]

Claudio and Don Pedro continue jesting until a challenge is finally given:

> **Claudio:** Nay then, give him another staff. This last was broke cross. [Since Benedick had referred to jousting, Claudio answers that Benedick needs another lance because he ineptly broke his "staff" on the last "charge."]
> **Don Pedro:** By this light, he changes more and more. I think he be angry indeed.
> **Claudio:** If he be, he knows how to turn his girdle. [Claudio may be referring to a wrestler turning his belt around as a signal to begin, or he may be advising Benedick to turn his belt so that his dagger or sword handle is within easy reach.]
> **Benedick:** Shall I speak a word in your ear?
> **Claudio:** God bless me from a challenge!

The war between Beatrice and Benedick is over, of course, by the time they declare their love for each other at the end of Act IV, Scene 1. The quotation above shows how the war imagery is continued, thus maintaining the tone that Claudio's denunciation of Hero created. The overall suggestiveness created by the imagery of war, battle, fencing, and charging, also reinforces the relationship between Beatrice and Benedick, which takes up a large portion of the play.

Question 16
How may Shakespeare's use of music and dance be considered part of his style?

Answer

It is generally acknowledged that music was loved in the Elizabethan age. Serious plays utilized instrumental accompaniment to intensify a mood; comedies were filled with songs and dancing; and many playwrights used music and dancing to heighten the element of spectacle.

In *Much Ado About Nothing*, Beatrice first advances the theme of rhythmic behavior in her famous "wooing, wedding and repenting" speech (Act II, Scene 1). The reference to dancing is immediately translated into action when the people in masks enter and the dance music strikes up. An actual dance in stately measure takes place on stage as the characters converse. Music is mentioned next in reference to the romantic characteristics of the conventional lover. This occurs (Act II, Scene 3) when Balthasar sings another song at the request of Don Pedro and Claudio (more music is to be sung that night under Hero's window). Notice how Benedick undercuts the praise Don Pedro gives Balthasar: "And he had been a dog that should have howled thus, they would have hanged him." There is also the punning on the word "notes," which again advances the concept of appearance versus reality, or any of the word's various meanings. Ironically, the song itself is about the inconstancy and deception of men. This, too, fits nicely with the deception Leonato, Don Pedro and Claudio are going to play on Benedick. Previously, Benedick had complained about Claudio's shifting from manly music to love songs as a sign of his having fallen in love. This motif will be repeated when Beatrice tells Hero she is only able to speak in the "sick tune" (Act III, Scene 4). Benedick also tries to sing a love song he has composed in the manner of a courtly lover, but must break off because the song is too commonplace. He also realizes he is no singer, and that he cannot woo in "festival terms" (Act V, Scene 3). The next scene shows Claudio in front of Hero's monument. He orders the musicians to play a specially composed elegy to be sung. The words of the song, about Hero's unfortunate death, are appropriate for the occasion. The last scene in the play ends with a bright dance and gay music.

*Comedy in *Much Ado About Nothing*

"In his comick scenes," said Dr. Johnson, "he seems to produce without labour what no labour can improve....His tragedy seems to be skill, his comedy to be instinct." Whatever applicability this may have to the tragedies of Shakespeare's prime, and it appears to have none at all, its truth is perhaps self-evident with respect to the three comedies he wrote during the last year or so of the sixteenth century. And it provides a convenient starting-point for any discussion of *Much Ado About Nothing*, whose comedy of Benedick and Beatrice is so flexible, so instinctive, and whose tragedy of Claudio and Hero is so strangely stiff.

If the last epithet is deserved there would seem to have been no skill employed in the painful tale of Leonato's daughter. Nor in its own terms can much be said for the sober plot which somewhat duskily weaves its web across the heart of an otherwise bright play. But in the strategy of the play as a whole much skill was used. A difficult problem had been posed, and it was more than satisfactorily solved. This does not mean that the Hero story would be convincing by itself or that the Beatrice story is substantial out of its context. It means that the two must be considered together; that Shakespeare did in fact consider them together, and did with ingenuity maintain them in a relation of mutual support. The problem was dual: how to prevent the main action, and indeed the only action, from turning the play into a tragedy or a near-tragedy; and how to bestow enough body upon the comic theme to make it matter either in itself or in its function as preventive. The result of Shakespeare's labor, most of which he concealed, is that Hero and Claudio never come close enough to us for pity or terror to be felt, and that Beatrice and Benedick, created as an insulating medium between tragedy and us, become finally so important as to bear all away upon their comic backs. But it is the seriousness of the central situation that sheds upon Benedick and Beatrice so much importance. As the play stands, neither pair of lovers can do without the other. Both skill and instinct are maneuvering every scene.

Much Ado begins and ends with Beatrice and Benedick, whose prose thus describes the circumference of Shakespeare's comic circle. The first interesting thing of which we hear is the "merry war" between the two; "they never meet," Leonato explains to Don Pedro's messenger whom Beatrice has so much bewildered, "but there's a skirmish of wit between them" (Act I, Scene 1, 63-4). Beatrice with her fine strong voice and her masculine humor has come in haste to hear the news of Benedick and others, but chiefly of Benedick; and in ad-

*Editor's title. From *Shakespeare*, by Mark Van Doren (New York: Henry Holt and Co., 1939).

vance of his arrival she has baited his name. In a few minutes he comes
swinging on and they are at it:

> Beatrice: I wonder that you will still be talking, Signior
> Benedick. Nobody marks you.
> Benedick: What, my dear Lady Disdain! are you yet living?
>
> (Act I, Scene 1, 117-20)

Even so early a tone is set for the play which the somber doings of
Hero and Claudio will find it difficult to destroy. A wall of brass-
bright words begins to be erected, a wall which terror perhaps will
never pierce. There is to be much talk for the sake of talk, and our experience of the theater leads us therefore to expect pure comedy. But a
conflicting note is struck at once, for the villain of such tragedy as we
shall have has arrived with Benedick; he is Don John, and his first
speech is a cold one. "I am not of many words" (Act I, Scene 1, 159).
Is the communication ominous? We do not know yet, for our attention
is immediately turned to the wager between Benedick and his friends.
Benedick is one of those spirited bachelors who ride high over love but
who for that very reason can fall with wonderful suddenness into its
arms. Don Pedro and Claudio, predicting his fall, prod him into
swearing that if it happens they can hang him in a bottle like a cat (Act
I, Scene 1, 259). Surely now there is nothing but comic stuff ahead;
Benedick, who already has admitted that Beatrice is beautiful except
for her fury (193-5), fools nobody, and least of all ourselves. We know
what will happen. We settle ourselves to see whether it is to be amus-
ingly worked out.

Here again, however, intrudes the cold, muffled voice of Don
John. "Let me be that I am" (Act I, Scene 3, 38), he mutters. That is
the accent of an unalterable villain. Furthermore, he is cynical about
marriage, for a man who would wed is one "that betroths himself to
unquietness" (Act I, Scene 3, 50). Yet we have just heard Benedick
deny that he is one to "sign away Sundays," and we are soon to hear
Beatrice thank God because he sends her no husband (Act II, Scene 1,
28-30); her hope of heaven is of a place where she can sit with the
bachelors and be as merry as the day is long. Don John's hatred of
love, however serious it may be, is stupidly stated and sounds harmless
in the envelope of banter into which Shakespeare has slipped it. The
plot nevertheless is thickening, and a complication potentially as grave
as that of "Othello," and indeed analogous to it, commences to
declare itself. Don Pedro, wooing Hero for Claudio at a masked ball,
acts his part so cleverly that Don John can make Claudio jealous at the
spectacle; and when nothing comes of this, for the lovers straighten the
matter out and are at once betrothed, there is the further threat to their

happiness of the window-plot which Don John and Borachio now disclose.

This is a serious threat, but before it is felt as real or dangerous a lighter fiction is hatched by the high-hearted persons of the play. It is in fact a pair of fictions, and Don Pedro, who wooed Hero so gaily for his friend, is at the bottom of both. Benedick and Beatrice are to be induced to fall in love with each other — or, since they already are in love, to confess that they are — by overhearing certain conversations prepared for the purpose. Each is to hear that the other is afflicted with love but is too proud to say so, being too sure that a confession would be scorned; each of them suffers in silence from the other's unthinking cruelty. Benedick and Beatrice, in other words, are to be turned into lovers by hearing themselves talked about — a common occurrence in the world, but they are not common. The ruse is sure to succeed, we want to see it succeed, and the play pauses while we do. There is no attempt on Shakespeare's part to complicate the business with plausible delays. The one charming scene follows hard upon the other; the lovers are converted schematically in turn; and a brisk vocabulary of sporting terms brightens and speeds this portion of the play. Benedick had likened Claudio, jealous of Don Pedro, to a poor hurt fowl creeping into sedges (Act II, Scene 1, 208-9), but he himself is now a fish on a hook (Act II, Scene 3, 113), a fowl to be stalked (Act II, Scene 3, 94); and Beatrice is a golden fish to be angled for (Act III, Scene 1, 26-7), a bird to be limed (Act III, Scene 1, 104), a lapwing who runs close to the ground to hear the ladies' conference (Act III, Scene 1, 24-5), a coy wild haggard of the rock (Act III, Scene 1, 35-6). The tone of comedy would seem then to be firmly set, not only by the prattle but by the kind of brittle action that belongs to comedy everywhere.

And it is very firmly set. *Much Ado* henceforth will be nothing if not comic. But its texture will be unique. For Benedick and Beatrice do not meet to confess their love until the threat to their friends' love has been made good; until the catastrophe of Claudio's denunciation has struck like lightning in the church; and until Hero is understood by him to be dead. Nothing of melodrama is remitted here, except that the villainy of Don John is narrated, not witnessed; and the words of Claudio about his rotten orange (Act IV, Scene 1, 33) are for the moment shocking. The disaster is swift and real enough for us to feel a difference in Benedick and Beatrice when they come together just after it to reap the harvest of their twin deceptions. For their relation has deepened under the strain; and once more there is something that prevents them from making love simply. The briefest declarations are followed by a sharp command from Beatrice:

Benedick: I protest I love you.
Beatrice: Why then, God forgive me!

Benedick: What offense, sweet Beatrice?

Beatrice:...I was about to protest I loved you.

Benedick: And do it with all thy heart.

Beatrice: I love you with so much of my heart that none is left to protest.

Benedick: Come, bid me do anything for thee.

Beatrice: Kill Claudio.

This introduces the sequence of events which leads up to Benedick's challenge of Claudio, and which lightens in tone to the point where the challenge is farcical — as farcical as old Antonio's whipping out his sword against Claudio (Act V, Scene 1). In itself, however, the dialogue is as rich in dramatic meaning as any in Shakespeare; the serious and the silly meet here in a marriage which the whole play thus far has conspired to arrange, and which the rest of it will subtly solemnize. Henceforth the persons central to the action will grow more and more like puppets, and the puppets of the comic byplay will grow more and more like persons. Hero will exist only as one who plays dead, and Claudio merely as one who mourns over an empty tomb. Benedick and Beatrice, even though they will never find time to make love simply, have all the future in their hands until Benedick shall send the audience home with "Strike up, pipers." Meanwhile the abused lady whose shadow falls on their dialogue and colors it to a brave tension will have done much for them; Hero it is who, whether she knows it or not, has given them their lofty position among Shakespeare's most interesting lovers.

Meanwhile as well there have been Dogberry, Verges, and the watch. If nothing else had directed the audience how to feel, and whether to feel deeply, the ineffable presence of these simpletons would have done so. Only a comedy could contain such harmless and irrelevant officials, such senseless and fit men for constables of a solemn watch. Their dunderheadedness remains indefinable; their nature is as resistant to analysis as that of the somehow sublime Bottom; and yet their destiny on any stage would be as clear as day. Their minds are muddy but their course is charted. They will blunder about in their tedious and stubborn "vigitance" till they have made all well. Fools like that cannot fail. What the wisdoms of gentlemen would never discover they bring to light, mopping about with their hiccups and their lanterns, and stumbling into the grace of our loud laughter. Benedick and Beatrice draw a clear circle of wit about the play to keep its tragedy in place. Dogberry and his fellows are a coarse tallow candle burning near the center, keeping the comic peace.

Talk is the business of *Much Ado*. Most of its merit is therefore in its prose, compared with which the verse is generally insignificant. An exception is the dialogue of Hero and Ursula while Beatrice listens like a lapwing close by the ground. The dialogue would be an exception if it contained no more than the one good line,

> Disdain and scorn ride sparkling in her eyes.
>
> (Act III, Scene 1, 51)

But it is crowded with good lines, as befits the sudden concentration of our interest in a scene where for once — and we shall find that it is only once — Beatrice stands exposed as the romantic young woman she is. Elsewhere she wears for protection the impenetrable veil of wit. That may make her still more romantic, but prose is the medium through which we should discover that this is so, for the economy of prose is irony's most faithful servant, and epigrams take best effect in something that sounds like conversation. Beatrice can scarcely be imagined in love with a man who is a poet all the time. Benedick never is. Finding himself in love he tries to show it in rhyme, but he can think of nothing better than "baby" to go with "lady," "horn" with "scorn," and "fool" with "school." "Very ominous endings," he concludes. "No, I was not born under a rhyming planet, nor I cannot woo in festival terms" (Act V, Scene 2, 40-1). He is of course not far distant from Hotspur, who with him helps to say for Shakespeare that verse, at any rate for the time being, seems limited as a channel when the full tide of life comes pouring through.

The prose of Benedick and Beatrice is a brilliant brocade of artifice. But its counterpoint of antithesis and epithet is natural to two such desperate defenders of pride against the leveling guns of love, of personality against passion. It is a logical language for persons who seldom say what they mean, and who, since they love nothing better than talk, must talk always for effect. It is the inevitable idiom for lovers who would deny their love.

> O, she misus'd me past the endurance of a block! An oak but with one green leaf on it would have answered her. My very visor began to assume life and scold with her. She told me, not thinking I had been myself, that I was the Prince's jester, that I was duller than a great thaw; huddling jest upon jest with such impossible conveyance upon me that I stood like a man at a mark, with a whole army shooting at me. She speaks poniards, and every word stabs. If her breath were as terrible as her terminations, there were no living near her; she would infect to the north star....Will your Grace command me any service to the world's end? I will go on the slightest errand now to the Antipodes that you can devise to send me on; I will fetch you a toothpicker now from the furthest inch of

Asia, bring you the length of Prester John's foot, fetch you a hair off the great Cham's beard, do you any embassage to the Pigmies, rather than hold three words' conference with this harpy.

(Act II, Scene 1, 246-79)

Benedick is a virtuoso in hyperbole, and is so much at home in the language of lies that he can make prose music, just for the fun of it, out of long words juxtaposed with short, out of rare silken terms thrust suddenly among russet yeas and noes. "With such impossible conveyance," "as terrible as her terminations," "do you any embassage" — this is the accent of Hamlet as he holds Rosencrantz and Guildenstern at the far end of his tongue, and it is the accent indeed of any gentleman in Shakespeare when his mind races ahead of his discourse. Benedick can be plain enough when he is alone, though even then he enjoys his voice and smiles at his brevity. "No, the word must be peopled. When I said I would die a bachelor, I did not think I should live till I were married" (Act II, Scene 3, 250-3).

Beatrice is "my Lady Tongue," and no better than Benedick can manage the art of keeping still. Don Pedro hits off her lover's loquacity when he remarks that "he hath a heart as sound as a bell and his tongue is the clapper, for what his heart thinks his tongue speaks" (Act III, Scene 2, 12-4). But it is usually Beatrice who makes the accusation, just as it is Benedick from whom we hear that Beatrice talks honest men to death. Both are right. Beatrice is so much in love with words that she can even be impatient with the silence of others. "Speak, count, 'tis your cue," she cries to Claudio when he stands tongue-tied before Hero at the betrothal. And "Speak, cousin," she cries in turn to Hero; "or, if you cannot, stop his mouth with a kiss" (Act II, Scene 1, 321-22). We shall remember this in the last scene when Benedick, listening to the fabulous lie she tells of having yielded to him only to save him from a consumption, all but ends the play with "Peace! I will stop your mouth," and kisses her soundly.

There is poetry in her repartee:

Don Pedro: In faith, lady, you have a merry heart.

Beatrice: Yea, my lord; I thank it, poor fool, it keeps on the windy side of care....I was born to speak all mirth and no matter....

Don Pedro: Out o' question, you were born in a merry hour.

Beatrice: No, sure, my lord, my mother cried; but then there was a star danc'd, and under that was I born.

(Act II, Scene 1, 325-50)

And there is sometimes a dash of indecency:

> **Don Pedro:** You have put him down, lady, you have put him down.
> **Beatrice:** So I would not he should do me, my lord, lest I should prove the mother of fools.   (Act II, Scene 1, 292-5)

"Neither his gentlemen nor his ladies," thought Dr. Johnson, "have much delicacy," and Shakespeare indeed made Benedick still franker. Their indelicacy sorts perfectly, as a matter of fact, with the suddenness of their poetry. Both are signs of their beautiful, unlimited power — a power whose existence we need to know in order that we may measure a love that must live without any other expression than the inverted one of raillery. There is never, perhaps, any doubt about this love. Beatrice in the first scene resents Benedick's new friend Claudio — "O Lord, he will hang upon him like a disease" (Act I, Scene 1, 86). And she is woefully let down when, going among the women for the first time after she has overheard their conference, she hints that she is in love and Margaret teases her by pretending to misunderstand (Act III, Scene 4). The wit of Benedick and his Lady Tongue is wonderful but it is after all transparent. It is almost never absent. Even when he humbles himself to say:

> Thou and I are too wise to woo peaceably, (Act V, Scene 2, 73)

she cannot let him rest without asking him how he knows *he* is wise. But we see through such wit as through a prism, and the love we behold is all the more convincing because of the refraction. If there is nothing more attractive in comedy than a picture of two brilliant persons in love against their will, then we shall like *Much Ado About Nothing* as much better than *The Taming of the Shrew* as it is a better play by a maturer playwright. And if this playwright, being Shakespeare, is near the height of his powers we shall expect in his hero and heroine that kind of excellence which sets a standard. So for all time it does — with Mirabell and Millamant waiting a century off to measure themselves and miss it by no finest hair of their white wigs.

*More Ado About Claudio and the Sources of the Play

In commenting on Shakespeare's handling of the theme of the slandered bride in *Much Ado about Nothing*, critics have produced by their harsh judgment of Claudio what may turn out to be the phenomenon of the slandered groom. In the most recent and comprehensive study, Professor Charles Prouty has followed Miss Nadine Page in lifting him from the hell to which he has been consigned for varying degrees of punishment from the early eighteenth century to a kind of historical purgatory where he cannot be condemned as an unworthy lover because he is no lover at all but a realistic young Elizabethan seeking a good match according to the mercenary standards of his age. The verdict against Claudio is time-honored, and the witnesses include the most impressive names in Shakespeare scholarship, and yet when the evidence is carefully sifted, it appears to have certain shortcomings. The tradition begins a little over a hundred years after the play was written with Charles Gildon's remarks in Rowe's edition (1709). His judgment, and to a large extent all subsequent judgments, seem to me to be based more on what Claudio does than on the interpretation which the text puts on his actions. This might be an adequate method for a dumb show, but in complex drama the action must be understood in the light of the interpretation put on it in the speeches of the characters. Modern critics have cited book and verse, but again this evidence in supporting the tradition seems to me to be open to the charge of undue selectivity and occasionally of subjectivity. The path is thorny, and espousing the lost cause of Claudio may be Quixotic, and proposing methods may partake of the unscientific arrogance of Bacon; yet Claudio's character seems to me a dark tower whose mystery can only be solved by departing from the traditional path.

If we are without contemporary interpretations of *Much Ado*, we are not without contemporary comment on the plot which Shakespeare used. In a certain sense the way in which each author handles the potentialities of the plot constitutes his comment on its significance, together with whatever comments he may add either as narrator or through the speeches of his characters, but beyond this we have for both Ariosto and Bandello external editorial commentary. I propose, then, to study Shakespeare's handling of certain basic elements of the plot against the background of a closely related group of sources and analogues in order to see what light such a comparison will throw on the character of Claudio. This is, of course, exactly what Professor

*From "More Ado About Claudio: An Acquittal for the Slandered Groom," by Kerby Neill. *Shakespeare Quarterly*, III (1952).

Prouty has done more broadly, but I find myself very far from some of his conclusions. With some temerity for a Baconian discussion of methods, I believe that in dealing comprehensively with the whole play he has not solved the problem of Claudio satisfactorily because he has not sufficiently isolated and abstracted the plot elements that bear on this specific problem. I have restricted myself here to the problem of what moral blame the hero incurs for believing the slander against his bride, because it is the belief in the slander, not the subsequent repudiation of Hero, which is the crux of the problem, and I am limiting this still further to a closely related group within each of the two major Renaissance versions of the story. These groups, which I have designated for convenience according to their fountainheads, are as follows: A Version: Ariosto (translated by Harington), Peter Beverly's *Ariodanto and Ieneura*, the Phedon episode in the *Faerie Queene*, II. iv. 12-36, and the anonymous play, *Partial Law*; B Version: Bandello, the embellished translation by Belleforest, and *Much Ado*.

I

Even though one may be derived from the other, these two versions of the story differ, as Professor Prouty has pointed out, in character, scene, and point of view. It is an historic irony in their development, however, that the A Version, which was most popular in England, had very little moral attached to it in the original, but after picking up considerable moral in the commentary it became an exemplum of intemperance in the *Faerie Queene*, while the B Version, which began with a definite moral well integrated with its basic motivation, culminated in the high comedy of Shakespeare with virtually none of its original moral left. The conflict between reason and passion, a basic tenet of Renaissance ethics, is an important factor in the motivation of the hero, and it is equally significant that Spenser developed this aspect of the story to furnish an exemplum and that Shakespeare neglected it here almost entirely, however much he may have recognized it throughout his plays.

Detailed summaries or reprints of the variants of both versions are readily accessible in Furness and Prouty, but it may be well here to recall the main elements of the two plots, both for convenience and to achieve a certain emphasis:

A Version (Ariosto)

Two adventuring brothers come to Scotland where one of them wins the king's favor and the love of the princess. The lovers plight their troth secretly because of the problem of winning parental consent to such an uneven match. A jealous duke slanders the princess to the hero and for proof arranges with the maid, who is in love with him, to dress in her mistress' clothes and throw a ladder down from her window. The hero and his brother are convinced when they see the two embracing in the window. The hero's death is reported after he has made an unsuccessful attempt to commit suicide and turned hermit. His brother then denounces the princess, who, according to Scottish law, must pay the death penalty unless a champion can defend her cause against the accuser. The hero returns in disguise to champion her cause against his own brother. In the meantime the maid who has been sent off to be murdered by the duke, is rescued and arrives in time to stop the fratricidal combat. After being mortally wounded, the duke confesses, and the hero and the heroine are happily united.

B Version (Bandello)

The hero, returning from the wars loaded with honors and favors by the prince, falls in love with the daughter of a decayed aristocrat and makes dishonorable love to her, is refused, and finally seeks her in honorable marriage but with some hesitation about a mésalliance. After their engagement his best friend, who is also in love with the lady, secretly sends a courtier to him who accuses her of unchastity. As ocular proof he sees a man enter a window of a decayed part of her father's palace and hears him mention, while the ladder is being placed, a former assignation with her. The hero is convinced and repudiates the engagement, and her family makes it appear that she has died of the shock. He then awakens to how improbable the proof was, his friend confesses, and overcome with grief he offers to make amends to the family. They arrange for him to marry a supposed sister who turns out to be his original bride. All are forgiven and happily united.

The fundamental conflict of both plots is the cruel dilemma in which the hero is placed: shall he trust in his lady or shall he believe the ocular proof of her guilt? On the surface it appears that his emotions tell him to trust his lady, but his reason tells him that seeing is believing. The reader or spectator, however, recognizes the fine irony in this because the reasonable thing is to trust in the lady and the emotionally deranged course is to believe in the proof. The paradox or chiasmus in the moral sphere suggests a tragic flaw which threatens the hero with disaster. The ocular proof, or deception, produces an emotional reaction which leads the hero to hatred or despair. In either case the ultimate conflict is between love of lady and love of self, and, in Carlyle's idiom, the impostor from without only succeeds because of the impostor within. Bandello makes all of this abundantly clear.

Phrased in more abstract terms the conflict is between the quality of the hero's love and the credibility of the proof of the slander, and it is the nature of these elements which distinguishes the two versions of the story more than the external incidents. In each version a different kind of love is in conflict with a different degree of proof. Since both the quality of the hero's love and his acceptance of the proof are aspects of his moral character, at this point plot and character, and literary analysis and ethical values all meet. A comparison, then, of the two versions and certain of their variants for the quality of the hero's love, the nature of the proof of the slander, and the result of the conflict between them should give us a significant picture of what meaning each author attached to the story and what moral judgment he passed on the main character. Against this background a re-examination of the text should enable us to see Claudio from a more Elizabethan viewpoint.

This basic plot formula is complicated by the difference in the social positions of the hero and the heroine. The situation is perennial, but it had special significance in Renaissance culture. In the A Version Ariodant, who is only an adventuring knight, is but half successful when he has won his lady's heart; he has the still greater obstacle of winning her hand from her father the king. The notes in Harington cite the proverb, "Better is a man without money, than money without a man," and devote half of the moral commentary to praise of Genevra for being willing to marry a worthy man who is beneath her rather than to seek a mercenary marriage. Peter Beverly makes Ariodant despair at the initial impossibility of being able to declare his love to a princess. This situation also gives an additional motive for keeping their love secret in the best courtly tradition. It is at this half-way point that they are separated by the deception, but both their problems are solved when Ariodant appears as her champion because the king has promised her hand to anyone who will defend her. In *Partial Law* the princess can eat her cake and have it too because her lover turns out to be a prince in disguise who conveniently inherits the crown at the denouement. In the B Version the relative social positions are reversed, but the situation has an equally important bearing on the story, especially on the motivation. Timbreo decides to marry Fenicia only after a great struggle with himself, and when it appears that she is a wanton, what he formerly thought was her virtue then appears as a mere trick to catch him in matrimony. On the other hand, his repudiation of her appears to everyone else as a mere device on his part to escape from a mésalliance.

The relative social position of the hero and the heroine, then, is an important and well-integrated part of the plot, and the reversal of this relationship further differentiates the two versions of the story. In following the A Version Spenser keeps the difference in rank but, curiously enough, eliminates its effect from the plot, and Shakespeare virtually removes the difference in social position altogether.

II

...Even though he has taken a number of externals from the B Version, Shakespeare departs from the tradition here by removing all trade of carnality from the hero's love. In the repudiation scene, when Leonato suggests that Claudio may have "made defeat of her virginity," Claudio replies:

> I never tempted her with word too large;
> But, as a brother to his sister, show'd
> Bashful sincerity and comely love.
>
> (Act IV, Scene 1, 53-55)

If anything, the bitterness of Claudio's denunciation of Hero shows an abhorrence of such carnality. He expresses his ideal when he says, "You seeme to me as Dian in her Orbe" (Act IV, Scene 1, 58), but his bitterness when he adds:

> But you are more intemperate in your blood,
> Than Venus, or those pamp'red animals,
> That rage in savage sensuality.
>
> (Act IV, Scene 1, 60-62)

The first effect of this change in the story is to remove the initial conflict, the hero's attempt on the heroine's virtue. The second effect is *to idealize Claudio even as he denounces the innocent Hero*. He remains as a good man, although deceived, but his literary ancestors in the B Version become open cynics about women, or perhaps it should be said they revert to type, but they do not show nobility of character during this trial although they do appear capable of it when they finally repent. At this moment, however, they show a hatred born of wounded pride.

In eliminating the social difference between hero and heroine, Shakespeare removes the second conflict, that within the mind of the hero whether or not to marry beneath him. On the other hand, the heroine is not raised to a higher position as in the A Version. This is particularly important because both Nadine Page and Professor Prouty have argued extensively in favor of the traditional theory that Claudio was making a mercenary match in which his affections were not engaged. The theory seems to me untenable. The general evidence for this theory consists in the mercenary background of Elizabethan upper class marriages, in Claudio's general behavior, especially his failure to measure up to the conventional romantic lovers such as Romeo, Anthony, and others, and most specifically in the line where he asks if Hero has a brother only to learn she is her father's only heir (Act I, Scene 1, 296) and two passing remarks by Leonato (Act II, Scene 1, 313-315; Act V, Scene 1, 299). Of all these arguments, the first is the most difficult either to accept or to refute. The necessity for a dower, however small, at all levels of society gives a mercenary touch to marriage according to romantic standards, but it does not seem to me that it is a valid corollary that love did not also enter into some marriages....First Claudio is deeply attracted to Hero, and *then* he inquires if she is the only heir. The argument from social custom seems to me to refute itself here. In an age of exceptionally mercenary marriages among some of the upper class, and in a tradition where all classes expected some dower, could a playwright expect a response from the audience, from the groundlings to the galleries, that was marked enough to make this passing remark establish the hero as a mercenary lover? Such a response seems to stem from nineteenth-century critics. A mere prudential remark of this kind would hardly make an Elizabethan audience think that Claudio was mercenary, and there is no further development in the text to support the idea. In context, with the bachelor attitude of Benedick already established, the audience might well use the bachelor rhetoric and say, "Now he's hooked." Hero is not represented as a great heiress, and Leonato's approval of the match (Act I, Scene 2, 21-25; Act II, Scene 1, 70-71; Act IV, Scene 1, 18) seems to indicate that the marriage was more advantageous to Hero than it was to Claudio. The situation seems simple enough in the text: Claudio does not find an heiress and then decide to marry her; he finds in his own words the "sweetest lady that ever I look'd on" (Act I, Scene 1, 190), and then tries to arrange a marriage with her according to Elizabethan custom.

The argument that Claudio is not in love because he fails to behave like Shakespeare's more romantic lovers seems to me to be a demand that Shakespeare should have written a different play. Claudio's part is not too large, and in most of the places where he might develop his own love affair, Shakespeare shifts the spotlight to Benedick and Beatrice. This will become increasingly evident as we examine the story further.

If Claudio's love is neither carnal nor mercenary, the question of its exact quality still remains. Structurally the dramatist must establish his character near the beginning of the exposition. Claudio is much smitten with Hero from the first, but he faces the problem of talking about her either to Benedick, whose barbed wit and enmity to love hardly recommend him as a confidant, or to Don Pedro, a prince, whose rank precludes him at this point from being an exact familiar although the interest he shows in Claudio's problems brings them very close together. Faced with this situation, Claudio is reasonably lo-quacious. He begins by cautiously asking Benedick's opinion, and he grows increasingly serious despite the unsympathetic replies. She is "a modest young lady" (Act I, Scene 1, 166); "Can the world buy such a jewel?" (Act I, Scene 1, 182); "She is the sweetest lady that ever I look'd on" (Act I, Scene 1, 190); and in reply to Benedick's scornful question of his intent to turn husband, he says, "I would scarce trust myself, though I had sworn the contrary, if Hero would be my wife" (Act I, Scene 1, 197-198). Certainly this hardly sounds mercenary. When Don Pedro enters, Claudio is more guarded, as befits the rela-tion between prince and subject, but Benedick accuses him at once of being in love. Claudio's reply to Don Pedro's praise of Hero, "You speak this to fetch me in" (Act I, Scene 1, 225), does not prove in its context that he is not in love with Hero. Given the situation of a young man confessing his feelings to a scornful bachelor and a prince whose views are still in doubt, it is readily understandable why he shows such caution. When he is left alone with Don Pedro, he is more frank, and when he finds him sympathetic, he explains how he fell in love, and he compliments Don Pedro on his attitude:

How sweetly you do minister to love
That know love's grief by his complexion!
(Act I, Scene 1, 314-315)

If this first scene has established anything, it seems to me that it has in-troduced a sensitive young man who has just fallen in love and, being a very proper young man and most anxious to succeed in his suit, has ob-tained the help of his prince in arranging a marriage with the sweetest lady that he ever looked on. An actor can, of course, play these lines in many other ways after reading through the repudiation scene, but not, it seems to me, without doing violence to the text.

The subsequent action appears to me to be in harmony with this introduction. When Claudio thinks Don Pedro has won Hero for himself, he is sick with jealousy. Benedick describes his condition, "Poor hurt fowl! now will he creep into sedges" (Act II, Scene 1, 209-210), and his condition is so obvious that Don Pedro asks why he is sad, and if not sad, sick. Beatrice interprets correctly that he is jealous (Act II, Scene 1, 298-306). Claudio's part is here supported by the interpretation of three other characters.

Even in the repudiation scene, the picture of Claudio as an ardent young lover is not destroyed. Leonato gives the key to how the scene was to be played when he describes it afterwards:

> Would the two princes lie? and Claudio lie,
> Who lov'd her so that, speaking of her foulness,
> Wash'd it with tears?
>
> (Act IV, Scene 1, 153-155)

The verbal means by which Claudio washed his accusations with tears was by establishing the pathos of the situation through a comparison of what Hero had seemed to him and what now she was apparently proven to be. The first part of this comparison simply confirms the interpretation I have already made of the first two acts of the play; the second part expresses the Elizabethan horror of carnality and suggests that the punishment fits the crime. Claudio says, "You seeme to me as Dian in her orb,/As chaste as is the bud ere it be blown" (Act IV, Scene 1, 58-59), and a little later:

> O Hero! What a Hero hadst thou been,
> If half thy outward graces had been plac'd
> About thy thoughts and counsels of thy heart!...
> For thee I'll lock up all the gates of love....
>
> (Act IV, Scene 1, 101-103, 106)

When Borachio confesses his crime, the ideal and the real are again brought together in the mind of Claudio, and he exclaims, "Sweet Hero, now thy image doth appear/In the rare semblance that I lov'd it first." (Act V, Scene 1, 259-260)

These references to Claudio's love for Hero continue to the very end of the play. Even the distinction between "love" and "like" which Claudio makes when he is first describing to Don Pedro how he fell in love, and which Professor Prouty cites as evidence that his affections were not engaged, are kept in the final scene where he tells his masked bride, "I am your husband if you like of me," and Hero, unmasking, replies, "And when you loved, you were my other husband" (Act V, Scene 4, 59-61). Against this accumulated evidence of self-characterization as well as that through Benedick, Don Pedro, Beatrice, and even Leonato and Hero, it seems to me that a passing reference to a possible dowry is insufficient to establish Claudio as a mercenary lover in the eyes of an Elizabethan audience. It is even very difficult to see how these passages can be integrated into the part unless Claudio is played sympathetically as a young lover. It seems to me that the late Professor Spencer was considerably understating the case when he wrote, "A good actor can make Claudio's youth, grief, and bewilderment sympathetic."

From this evidence it appears that Claudio's love is neither carnal nor mercenary, and if not of that romantic extreme found in Ariodant or Romeo or Antony, yet he still remains as a man in love, and the audience might call this "real" or "romantic" or give it whatever term they wished to describe a man whose affections are deeply moved towards a woman who seemed to fulfill his high ideal, one who seemed as Diana in her orb and was also the sweetest lady he ever looked on.

III

...The crux of Shakespeare's handling of the character of Claudio is found in the way in which he met the problem of the proof. If he had continued to follow the B Version, then Claudio would have been much to blame for believing such an obvious slander against his lady, even as Timbreo is blamed, but instead he drew on the A Version for some materials and added others of his own in order to make the proof so strong that it tends to transfer the blame from the hero to the villain who perpetrated the whole plot. His first addition was the substitution of Don John, the Bastard, for the rival lover who, from an Elizabethan viewpoint, provided a stock character (Prouty, p. 34) black enough to carry the responsibility for all the acts of those who came under his influence. This dramatic convention is enough to compensate for the fact that in absolute terms he was not so reputable a witness as the duke in the A Version. Shakespeare's second addition was the strengthening of the verbal proof by substituting for an overheard remark an overheard conversation in which the maid is called by her lady's name (Act III, Scene 3, 153-155), and the false confession of Borachio (Act IV, Scene 1, 93-95). From the A Version he took the disguised maid and the witness (here Don Pedro) who largely removes the theme of self-deception from the story. In brief, Shakespeare has made the proof stronger than any other author in either the A or the B tradition, with the possible exception of Spenser, who, incidentally, does it to point a sterner moral; Shakespeare, however, uses the same device largely to eliminate such a moral by transferring the blame to the villain. Portraying a higher type of love than that found in the B Version, his plot required him to furnish stronger proof. Since, except for the two details mentioned above, the A Version has been discounted as a source, it is interesting to note that in the abstract Shakespeare has the same conflict as the A Version: a high degree of love in conflict with a high degree of proof....

Shakespeare's Claudio shows neither the high romanticism of Ariodant nor the realistic self-conceit of Timbreo. The truth is that his character has been more developed by the critics than it was by Shakespeare. There is some suggestion of an inner weakness when Borachio outlines the plot to Don John and concludes, "Then shall appear such seeming truth of Hero's disloyalty, that jealousy shall be call'd assurance, and all the preparation overthrown" (Act II, Scene 2, 48-51). This suggestion, however, is not developed. Claudio and Don Pedro, after a brief expression of doubt, half believe the slander from the beginning, and Claudio even announces his plan to repudiate Hero if the slander can be proved. There is no development of the doubts that are found in both Ariodant and Timbreo in the other versions. Such doubts and final belief in her innocence are found in Leonato who, with Antonio, Benedick, Beatrice, and the Friar, furnish a slight foil for Claudio's and Don Pedro's belief in her guilt; but little is made of it, and, even in the scene where Benedick challenges Claudio, the emphasis is on the subplot. The only scene where Claudio's part is allowed any emotional range is in the repudiation of Hero, where he washes his accusations with his tears. This is also the only place where he shows any real inner conflict. Even in the final scene when he is happily united to Hero, Benedick and Beatrice at once take over the prominence which might have been given to the main plot.

IV

When we turn to the final problem, the question of the moral blame attributed to Claudio for his belief in the slander against Hero and his subsequent repudiation of her, we find that the text allows him to go scot free. This is another aspect of the lack of development of his character. If there is no sin, there is no repentance. He says himself that he will accept "what penance your invention/Can lay upon my sin. Yet sinn'd I not/But in mistaking," and Don Pedro supports him, "By my soul, nor I!" (Act V, Scene 1, 283-284). The final whitewash comes from Leonato when, to the opening speech of the Friar in Scene 4 he replies,

> So are the Prince and Claudio, who accus'd her
> Upon the error that you heard debated.
> But Margaret was in some fault for this....
> (Act V, Scene 4, 2-5)

Neither the characters themselves nor Leonato, the aggrieved party who challenged the other two to a duel, admit that anyone has sinned except Don John, Borachio, and to some degree Margaret. Neither Ariodant in the A Version, who was willing to fight his brother and sacrifice his life for his lady even after the proof, nor Timbreo in the B Version, who so thoroughly acknowledged his fault, is so completely forgiven and whitewashed as Claudio is by the end of the play. But time has reversed Shakespeare's judgment and, whereas Ariodant and Timbreo are still adjudged to have a quality of the heroic about them, commentators have rendered Claudio an unmerciful cad, or, perhaps, on more considered judgment, the slandered groom.

Apart from these places in the text, it seems to me that Claudio was a sympathetic character to the Elizabethans through association, a device similar to the modern method of psychological zoning of the stage. Evil must be purged from the play, and it would seem that Shakespeare eliminates it by associating it with Don John. The late Professor Spencer advanced the theory that Don John was the fundamental weakness of the play, but it appears to me that he is the salvation of the otherwise mutilated main plot. Professor Harbage points out that his bastardy "carries with it a presumption of separation from normal men and their virtues," and Professor Prouty has suggested his Machiavellian background. He is a self-confessed villain from whom evil may be expected and to whom evil should be attributed. Even before the plot has been discovered, Benedick suspects him and tends to exonerate Don Pedro and Claudio:

> **Fri:** There is some strange misprision in the princes.
> **Ben:** Two of them have the very bent of honour;
> And if their wisdoms be misled in this,
> The practice of it lives in John the bastard,
> Whose spirits toil in frame of villainies.
> (Act IV, Scene 1, 186-190)

The very fact that he devises the most credible plot in any version tends to transfer the blame from the deceived Claudio to the contrivers of the deception. The plot is kept sufficiently before the audience and is early discovered by Dogberry, so the audience is always conscious both of the villainy of it and of the fact that Claudio's repudiation of Hero will only be temporary. Finally, the flight of Don John is mentioned four times (Act V, Scene 1, 192-193, 258; Scene 2, 100-102; Scene 4, 127), and this is almost symbolic of the purging of evil from the happy ending of the comedy.

Claudio is positively allied to the side of good by his association with the Prince, Don Pedro, who is almost his alter ego. He both woos for him and repudiates the lady with him, so that any blame that attaches to Claudio must also attach to Don Pedro. He is, like Claudio, the very bent of honor, and in addition he is one who sweetly ministers to love. He brings Claudio to Hero, Benedick to Beatrice, and in general plays the royal Cupid in the plot. He has the Elizabethan divinity that hedges a king, and he is cleared of all blame in the same breath with Claudio. By linking Claudio's denunciation of Hero with his royal patron, Shakespeare has virtually placed the entire action above criticism. There is a slight hint that his emotions might be engaged because his honor is at stake (Act II, Scene 2, 36-37), but it is no more developed than the fact of Claudio's jealousy being called assurance. Furthermore, the royal half-brothers represent the conflicting forces of good and evil: Don John, the bastard, tries to separate the lovers, that is, to hinder the action of the play; Don Pedro, the Prince, tries to bring both sets of young lovers together. The worst we can say of Don Pedro is that after magnanimously forgiving his brother for rising against him, he permits himself to be ungratefully deceived by the villain for a brief time.

In these broad terms Shakespeare has kept some integrity in the main plot, but he has removed all the nuances of character and the subtleties of structure that were in his sources. It is clear also that, although he took most of his externals from the B Version, he drew upon the A Version for the larger elements of the conflict — the type of love, the degree of proof, and the punishment of evil — but he did not attach the same meaning to these elements that the other authors and commentators did. In the B Version Timbreo is overcredulous. He says so himself, and the narrator's voice says so, the commentary says so, and the embellished version of Belleforest says so. In the A Version Ariodant is guilty, according to Harington's notes, of "credulous jealousy," in Beverly of a "faithles hart," and in Spenser of "wrath, gelosie, and grief," but in Shakespeare Claudio is free of all blame. I believe one reason is that he was not destined to play the major role in the play.

There is a larger conclusion that may be hazarded from the evidence of this comparative study of one aspect of the story. It has frequently been said that Shakespeare uses one plot as a background for another one, and that *Much Ado* is an example of this. To reduce a plot to a mere background, it is necessary to take some of the interest out of it. In both the A and the B Versions, the hero plays a good emotional part, his motivation is well-integrated with the plot, his friend and rival is a well-motivated complex character, and the story as a whole has adequate causality to give it unity. On the other hand, the character of Claudio has few dramatic possibilities outside of the repudiation scene, and as a result the great actors have generally played the part of Benedick. At every point where the hero's character is developed in either the A or the B Versions by showing his doubts, his fears, his regrets, or his misery, Shakespeare has eliminated Claudio from the spotlight and filled the interval with the affairs of Beatrice and Benedick. The discovery of the plot, as has often been pointed out, is by the blundering chance of Dogberry, not from reason awakening in the hero or repentance bringing the rival to a dramatic confession with his breast bared for the dagger of the wronged hero. In brief, all those developments which made an interesting and well-integrated plot have been omitted by Shakespeare in order to develop the sub-plot. Even at the very end where Hero unmasks, the happy Claudio turns at once to a consideration, not of his own affairs, but to those of Benedick. Even the use of the technique of association, a fairly general stage effect, tends to reduce the main plot to a backdrop for the subplot. If we were to consider Shakespeare's handling of the main plot alone, we would be forced to say that he butchered it; but when we consider the total play, we can see that he has very skilfully reduced it to a background for another story. The thematic unity, the use of the device of eavesdropping, the problem of marriage and cuckoldom, the harmonizing of the three levels of the play, the effect of the changes in the main plot on these things is beyond the scope of this study. I have limited myself to rehabilitating Claudio as a sympathetic hero, in short, to showing that he is the slandered groom. An additional conclusion to this material seems to be the paradoxical one that the subplot is really the main plot, and that the main plot is only the background. If I may hazard a guess as to why Shakespeare used this plot, regardless of whether he revised an old play or wrote a new one, it seems to me that the popularity of the theme was sufficient reason both for using it and for putting it in the background. In Professor Prouty's words, it was old hat.

*Elements of Plot in
Much Ado About Nothing

When Shakespeare wrote *Much Ado about Nothing* he had lost none of his skill as a maker of plots; on the contrary, he had attained further mastery in the ten years or more since the writing of *The Comedy of Errors*. There are three main narrative-lines: that of Claudio, Hero, and the wicked Don John; the connected story of Dogberry and the Watch; and the contrasting story of Beatrice and Benedick, all interwoven with clarity and apparent ease. But in this play Shakespeare uses the plot for a further and deeper end. Each of the three narrative-lines has its own humor, and by the interplay of the three a more general vision of man as laughable is suggested: a vision which is at once comic and poetic.

The story of young Claudio and Hero caught in Don John's wicked schemes was Shakespeare's starting point, and the somewhat casual framework of the plot of the whole play. He had read this story in Bandello's version, *Timbreo di Cardona*, the story of a girl unjustly accused of adultery. This tale, though it ends happily, is not very funny in itself, and Shakespeare does not so much avoid its painful and pathetic aspects as absorb them in his more detached comic vision. The scene in the church, when poor Hero is wrongly accused and her father Leonato loudly laments, may be played for a "tragic" effect, but that I think would not be quite right. The audience knows that it is all a mistake, and it is by that time accustomed to smile at Claudio, an absurdly solemn victim of young love's egoism. When he first appears he tries to tell the Duke what the Duke knew already: his all-important love for Hero. He glumly decides that the Duke, wooing Hero in his behalf, has stolen her, and so is wrong again. Beatrice labels him for us: "glum as an orange, and something of that jealous complexion." His false accusation is his third mistake: we must sympathize, but at the same time smile, at this final instance of his foolishness. The whole Claudio-Hero story is comic in itself and in its own way, but to understand what Shakespeare meant by it it is necessary to think of it in relation to the two other stories which unfold in alternation with it.

Dogberry and the Watch are closely connected with the Claudio story, which requires someone to uncover Don John's plot, but Shakespeare developed this element into a farcical sequence with its own tone and interest. At the same time he uses it to lighten the catastrophe at Hero's wedding, and the character of Don John: we cannot take a villain seriously who can be apprehended by Dogberry. Dogberry is not suffering the delusions of young love, like Claudio,

*Editor's title. From *The Human Image in Dramatic Literature* by Francis Fergusson (New York: Anchor Books, 1957).

but those of vanity and uncontrollable verbosity. His efforts to find his way, with lanterns, through the darkness of the night and the more impenetrable darkness of his wits, forms an ironic parallel to the groping of the young lovers through their mists of feeling. Dogberry also has his version of the underlying mood of the play — that of a leisurely and joyful ease, such as we attribute to Eden or the Golden Age. In Dogberry this infatuated leisureliness, this delusion that nothing terrible can really happen, takes the form of interminable verbalizing while the evil plot hatches and the villains lurk uncaught.

The story of Beatrice and Benedick's self-tormented love affair is entirely Shakespeare's creation. He seems to have felt the need of that pair's intelligence and agility to ventilate Claudio and Hero. We should tire quickly of Claudio's total submersion in love if Benedick were not there, pretending to be too intelligent for that. Hero, who can only sigh and blush, would be too soggy without Beatrice, who can only make sharp remarks, pull pigtails, and stick her tongue out at the boys. But the two contrasting stories together suggest a vision of early infatuation — provided we don't take Shakespeare's characters more seriously than he intended — which is both deeper and more comic than the victims themselves can know.

Beatrice and Benedick are notoriously hard to act on the modern stage, especially in the first two acts, where they indulge in so many quibbles and conceits in the taste of their times. There is no use trying to make the verbal jokes funny; but I am not sure that Shakespeare himself took them seriously as jokes. I once had the pleasure of seeing John Gielgud and Pamela Brown act several of the Beatrice-Benedick scenes. They "threw away" the words, or even, at moments, made fun of their far-fetched elaboration, and by this means focused their audience's attention on the noble, silly, intelligent and bewildered *relation* of the two — a relation as agile, musical, and deeply comic as that of Congreve's reluctant lovers, Mirabel and Millamant. I feel sure that this approach to the play is right: its surfaces, its literal words, characters and events, are not to be taken seriously: the point is in the music of unseen motivation, in the fact that it *is* unseen by the characters themselves — and that all the fun and folly plays against a background of mystery.

The main Claudio-Hero-Don John intrigue is also not to be taken too seriously, as though it were the point of the play: Shakespeare gets it under way casually, after the underlying mood of the play as a whole, and its "action" of elaborate play, or leisurely enjoyment, has been firmly established. The opening scene, in which Leonato's household prepares to celebrate the return of the Duke, Benedick and Claudio from their comic-opera war, tells us what the play is really about: it is a festive occasion, a celebration of a certain evanescent but recurrent human experience. The experience is real in its way, all may recognize it, but under its spell everything the characters do is much ado about nothing. The progress of the underlying action of the play as a whole is therefore marked by a series of somewhat dreamy and deluded festive occasions. The first of these is Leonato's masked ball, in Act II, a visible and musical image of the action. Then comes Dogberry's nocturnal and incomprehensible charge to the Watch: a farcical version of the theme. The fourth act consists chiefly of the marriage which turns out to be no marriage at all, but a bad dream. In the fifth act there is Claudio's funeral tribute to Hero, by night, at her supposed tomb; but this is a funeral which is no funeral, corresponding to the marriage which was no marriage. After that pathetic and comic expiatory rite, daylight returns, the torches are put out, and we are ready for the real and double marriage, in daylight, with the ladies unmasked at last, which ends the play in dance and song.

We are just beginning to understand the technical value of the "ceremonious occasion" as an element of plot, though it has been used in countless ways from Aristophanes to Henry James. When people assemble for a ceremonious occasion (whether it be the festival of Dionysos or one of James's thorny tea parties) they must abate, or conceal, their purely individual purposes, and recognize the common concern which brings them together. A dramatist may use the festive occasion, therefore, to shift his audience's attention from the detail of the literal intrigue to some general plight which all more or less unwittingly share. All are social and political animals; all must suffer spring, mating, and death. Ceremonious occasions are especially useful to dramatists who are seeking poetry, which, as Aristotle remarked, is concerned with something more general than the particular facts, the unique events, of human life. The point — the comic point — of *Much Ado* — is poetic in that sense, and hence it is the festive ensemble scenes which most clearly adumbrate the basic vision of the play. In this respect the plot of *Much Ado* contrasts sharply with that of *The Comedy of Errors*. The point of that play lies precisely in the unique situation of mistaken identity, and in the strings of absurd events which quickly follow from it. An "occasion" of any kind would break the tight concatenation of *contretemps*; and that Shakespeare is careful to avoid doing until he is ready to end the whole play.

One might say that *Much Ado* presents a comic vision of mankind which is also poetic, while the purpose of *The Comedy of Errors* is closer to that of the professional vaudevillian, who gauges his success by clocking the laughs: the provoking of thoughtless mirth, an almost reflex response. The difference between the two plays is clearest, perhaps, when one reflects that both are concerned with mistaken identity, but in *The Comedy of Errors* the mistake is simply a mistake in fact, while in *Much Ado* it is a failure of insight, or rather many failures of different kinds by the different characters.

Shakespeare accomplishes the *dénouement* of *The Comedy of Errors* in one swift scene. It is not difficult to correct an error in fact: it may be done instantly by providing the right fact: and as soon as both pairs of twins are on stage together, the error is gone. But correcting a failure of insight is a most delicate and mysterious process, which Shakespeare suggests, in *Much Ado*, in countless ways: through the symbolism of masks, night, and verbal ambiguities, and in peripeteias of his three variously comic subplots.

The farcical efforts of Dogberry and Verges never deviate into enlightenment. They learn as little as the characters in *The Comedy of Errors*: but, like them, they do stumble eventually upon the right fact: they manage to apprehend the villains and convey that fact to Leonato.

Claudio, with his dark fumes of love, has a long way to go before he can see anything real. After his false wedding Shakespeare puts him through a false and painful challenge from his best friend, Benedick, and then the mocking (but touching) mummery of his visit to Hero's empty tomb. Even then the audience learns more from Claudio's masquerade-like progress through the maze than he does himself.

Beatrice and Benedick come the closest, of all the characters, to grasping the whole scope of the comic vision which the play slowly unfolds. But even after their friends have tried to kid them out of their frightened vanity during the first three acts, it takes most of the fourth and fifth acts, where all the painful things occur, to bring them to conscious acceptance of their absurd selves, each other, and their love. It is the fiasco of Claudio's first attempt at marriage which marks the crucial turn in their relationship:

Benedick: Lady Beatrice, have you wept all this while?
Beatrice: Yea, and I will weep a while longer.

and a little later:

Benedick: I do love nothing in the world so well as you. Is not that strange?
Beatrice: As strange as the thing I know not. It were as possible for me to say I love nothing so well as you; but believe me not; and yet I lie not; I confess nothing....

In this exchange the love-warmed final scene of the play is foreshadowed, but the misfortunes of Claudio and Hero, which here bring Beatrice and Benedick near together, immediately carry them apart again. Benedick has to challenge Claudio, and that boy's delusions have to be repented and dispelled, before Beatrice and Benedick can trust their intuition of love, or accept it fully and in good conscience. I do not attempt to follow the subtle shifts in their relationship which Shakespeare suggests, in a few quick, sure strokes, during the fifth act. But it is Beatrice and Benedick who dominate the final scene:

> **Benedick:** Soft and fair, Friar. Which is Beatrice?
> **Beatrice** (*unmasking*): I answer to that name. What is your will?
> **Benedick:** Do not you love me?
> **Beatrice:** Why no, no more than reason.
> **Benedick:** Why then, your uncle and the Prince and Claudio have been deceived; they swore you did.
> **Beatrice:** Do not you love me?
> **Benedick:** Troth no, no more than reason.
> **Beatrice:** Why then my cousin, Margaret, and Ursula are much deceived, for they did swear you did.

(Claudio and Hero produce love letters from Benedick and Beatrice to each other.)

> **Benedick:** A miracle! here's our own hands against our hearts. Come, I will have thee; but, by this light, I take thee for pity.
> **Beatrice:** I would not deny you, but by this good day I yield upon great persuasion, and partly to save your life, for I was told you were in a consumption.
> **Benedick:** Peace; I will stop your mouth.

In this scene the main contrasting themes of the play are brought together, and very lightly and quickly resolved: marriage true and false, masking and unmasking, the delusion and truth of youthful love. The harmonies may all be heard in Beatrice's and Benedick's words. The exchange is in prose, but (like the prose of Leonato's masked ball) it has a rhythm and a varied symmetry suggesting the formality of a dance figure. The key words — love, reason, day, light, pity, peace — make music both for the ear and for the understanding as they echo back and forth, deepening in meaning with each new context. The effect of the scene as a whole is epitomized in Beatrice's and Benedick's heavenly double-take: their foolish idiosyncrasy is clear, but some joyful flood of acceptance and understanding frees them, for the moment, and lifts them beyond it. Is this effect "comic"? I do not know; I think it is intended to bring a smile, not for the windup of this little plot, but for the precarious human condition.

When one reads *Much Ado* in the security of one's own room, indulging in daydreams of an ideal performance, it is possible to forget the practical and critical problems which surround the question of the play's viability in our time. But it must be admitted that high school productions are likely to be terribly embarrassing, and I do not even like to think of the play's pathetic vulnerability on Times Square. The play demands much from its performers, almost as much as Chekhov does. It demands a great deal from its audience: a leisurely and contemplative detachment which seems too costly in our hustled age. Perhaps Shakespeare should be blamed for all this: if *Much Ado* does not easily convince us on the contemporary stage, perhaps we should conclude, as Eliot once concluded of *Hamlet*, that it is an artistic failure. But on that principle we should have to rule out a great deal of Shakespeare. It was his habit, not only in *Hamlet* and *Much Ado*, but in many other plays, to indicate, rather than explicitly to present, his central theme; and to leave it to his performers and his audience to find it behind the varied episodes, characters, and modes of language which are literally presented. Everything which Shakespeare meant by *The Comedy of Errors* is immediately perceptible; the comic vision of *Much Ado* will only appear, like the faces which Dante saw in the milky substance of the moon, slowly, and as we learn to trust the fact that it is really there.

Selected Criticisms

Much Ado About Nothing is saturated with [the] idea of the power of Nothing (of the creative ingredient of the imagination, that is) to alter the nature of things for good or ill, for, as Shakespeare's History Plays so abundantly show, fear and hate, as well as faith and love, have the capacity to attract facts to them and so, temporarily at least, to confirm their own hypotheses. But the changes of fear and hate effect are destructive and pointed in the direction of chaos, whereas imagination integrates, makes for synthesis and reconciliation of clashing interests. The play is full of phrases that imply this fluidity of facts, their willingness to flow for good or evil into any mold the human mind makes for their reception. Antonio brings news to Leonato. "Are they good?" asks the latter. "As the event stamps them," the former replies. "You have of late stood out against your brother," says Conrade to Don John, "and he hath ta'en you newly into his grace; where it is impossible you should take true root but by the fair weather that you make yourself: it is needful that you frame the season for your own harvest." The children of this world, as Jesus divines, are often wiser in these matters than the children of light. But not so in the case of Friar Francis. "Die to live," is his advice to Hero, which is only a more succinct summary of his prophecy of the effect on Claudio of the "nothing" of Hero's death:

> for it so falls out
> That what we have we prize not to the worth
> Whiles we enjoy it, but being lack'd and lost,
> Why, then we rack the value, then we find
> The virtue that possession would not show us
> Whiles it was ours. So will it fare with Claudio:
> When he shall hear she died upon his words,
> The idea of her life shall sweetly creep
> Into his study of imagination
> And every lovely organ of her life
> Shall come apparell'd in more precious habit,
> More moving-delicate, and full of life
> Into the eye and prospect of his soul,
> Than when she liv'd indeed.

Harold C. Goddard

Richard Grant White's suggestion, made as long ago as 1857, that *nothing* and *noting* constituted an Elizabethan pun has recently been seconded in Kökeritz's valuable study of Elizabethan pronunciation. Kökeritz, however, considers it "unlikely" that *noting* is used to mean eavesdropping, as White had further suggested. In the words of Professor Jorgensen, "rejection" of this latter portion of the early critic's theory is "implicit" in the "almost perfect editorial silence" that followed it. Commentators on the play have been content to point to the repeated use of eavesdropping and leave the matter there. But noting in a sense understood today as well as in Shakespeare's day is, I believe, the key to the play's thematic unity — *noting* meaning to observe or, as Schmidt cites it in his *Lexicon*, "to attend to, to observe" (II, 780-781). We note a situation; we take note of a situation — we see and hear, then judge and act accordingly. *Much Ado* is a comedy of *mis*-noting in this common sense. Eavesdropping, then, becomes just one kind of observation. Throughout the play every character is required to observe and judge, and almost every character judges poorly. Deception plays a part in these misjudgments, as Professor Prouty has pointed out, but much more pervasive a force is a common human frailty — the inability to observe, judge, and act sensibly. The play, then, is a dramatization of mis-noting — a sort of dramatized, rather than verbal, pun.

· · ·

Shakespeare signals his purpose in another way, too, the verbal pun. In his opening scene when Claudio asks his friend, "Benedick, dids't thou note the daughter of Signior Leonato?" (1. 164), he prompts this reply, "I noted her not, but I look'd on her" (1. 165). A more striking use of the verbal pun occurs, of course, in the dialogue between Balthazar, the singer, and Don Pedro in Act II, Scene 3. To end Balthazar's polite noises about his poor voice, Don Pedro bids him

> Nay, pray thee come:
> Or if thou wilt hold longer argument,
> Do it in notes.
> **Balth:** Note this before my notes:
> There's not a note of mine that's worth the noting.
> **Pedro:** Why, these are very crotchets that he speaks!
> Notes notes, forsooth, and nothing!   (Act II, Scene 3, 54-60)

The textual difficulty of the last word is of little consequence at this moment. Whether Shakespeare wrote *nothing* or *noting*, the entire passage emphasizes the word *note* unquestionably, punning on the musical term and the idea of observing or heeding. The placing of this dialogue is interesting, too, for Shakespeare chooses the moment of Benedick's gulling for thus calling our attention once more to his thematic device of noting.

Dorothy C. Hockey

Without striving to make too much of it, the dance in Act II, Scene 1 is beautifully apposite. The couples walk their round, two by two, all masked; and all are using words to back the disguise of false faces with trivial deceit. The play-acted defamation of Hero, by means of a false dress on the wrong woman and names used falsely, is exactly parallel. In both, the truth is *behind* the looks and words. The *bal masqué* is only a game of seeming; yet it is a most apt symbol of the whole. The vizor is half deceit, half no deceit: you can never be sure. Believe it, and you make ado about what is nothing. And in the social order and shared delight of the dance — all moving to the controlling rhythm, in their appointed patterns — there is too the emblem of the harmony in which all will conclude: as the play does, with another dance, all the vizors laid aside. The real play is not ended with "Strike up, pipers." The very movement of Act II, Scene 1, where all the main misapprehensions started, is repeated and completed; and even the professed misogamists are dancing to the same tune. It is as neat and pretty as "Sigh no more, ladies, sigh no more."

A.P. Rossiter

The scene [Act II, Scene 3] opens with Benedick laughing at the thought of the lovesick Claudio and congratulating himself on being heart-whole, and he expresses their contrasted states in musical imagery.

> I have known him when there was no music in him, but the drum and the fife; and now had he rather hear the tabor and the pipe....Is it not strange that sheeps' guts should hale souls out of men's bodies? — Well, a horn for my money when all's done.

We, of course, know that Benedick is not as heart-whole as he is trying to pretend. Beatrice and Benedick resist each other because, being both proud and intelligent, they do not wish to be the helpless slaves of emotion or, worse, to become what they have often observed in others, the victims of an imaginary passion. Yet whatever he may say against music, Benedick does not go away, but stays and listens.

Claudio, for his part, wishes to hear music because he is in a dreamy, lovesick state, and one can guess that his *petit roman* as he listens will be of himself as the ever-faithful swain, so that he will not notice that the mood and words of the song are in complete contrast to his daydream. For the song is actually about the irresponsibility of men and the folly of women taking them seriously, and recommends as an antidote good humor and common sense. If one imagines these sentiments being the expression of a character, the only character they suit is Beatrice.

She is never sad but when she sleeps; and not even sad then; for I have heard my daughter say, she hath often dream'd of happiness and waked herself with laughing. She cannot endure hear tell of a husband. Leonato by no means: she mocks all her wooers out of suit.

I do not think it too far-fetched to imagine that the song arouses in Benedick's mind an image of Beatrice, the tenderness of which alarms him. The violence of his comments when the song is over is suspicious:

I pray God, his bad voice bode no mischief! I had as lief have heard the night-raven, come what plague could have come after it.

And, of course, there *is* mischief brewing. Almost immediately he overhears the planned conversation of Claudio and Don Pedro, and it has its intended effect. The song may not have compelled his capitulation, but it has certainly softened him up.

More mischief comes to Claudio who, two scenes later, shows himself all too willing to believe Don John's slander before he has been shown even false evidence, and declares that, if it should prove true, he will shame Hero in public. Had his love for Hero been all he imagined it to be, he would have laughed in Don John's face and believed Hero's assertion of her innocence, despite apparent evidence to the contrary, as immediately as her cousin does. He falls into the trap set for him because as yet he is less a lover than a man in love with love. Hero is as yet more an image in his own mind than a real person, and such images are susceptible to every suggestion.

For Claudio, the song marks the moment when his pleasant illusions about himself as a lover are at their highest. Before he can really listen to music he must be cured of imaginary listening, and the cure lies through the disharmonious experiences of passion and guilt.

W.H. Auden

The imagery of *Much Ado* can be separated from the action only by an act of violence, so much is it a part of the texture of the play. This is particularly true of the predominant imagery, that of fashion, a natural vehicle for the controlling theme. Shakespeare makes a much more extensive use of fashion imagery here than in any other play. What is more interesting is the deliberate emphasis given this imagery: all the uses may be regarded as masking other meanings. Some of these images may arise from a fortuitous association of ideas on the author's part, particularly when they occur in isolated sentences, as when Beatrice says that Benedick "wears his faith but as the fashion of his hat; it ever changes with the next block" (Act I, Scene 1, 75-77). But the main uses are integrated with the action itself. Thus one of the marks of Claudio's newly discovered love for Hero is his interest in fashions (Act II, Scene 3, 15-19). Benedick is likewise betrayed as a lover by his sudden fancy for strange disguises:

> **Pedro:** There is no appearance of fancy in him, unless it be a fancy that he hath to strange disguises; as to be a Dutchman today, a Frenchman tomorrow; or in the shape of two countries at once, as a German from the waist downward, all slops, and a Spaniard from the hip upward, no doublet. Unless he have a fancy to this foolery, as it appears he hath, he is no fool for fancy, as you would have it appear he is.
>
> (Act III, Scene 2, 31-39)

Obviously both of these uses should be reflected in the costuming of the actors. Fashion is not merely a cluster of images here; with its associated images of the cut beard, washed face, perfume, and paint (ii. 42-59), it is the substance of the main part of the scene, occupying the minds of Leonato, Don Pedro, and Claudio: the gentlemen conclude from the outward signs of Benedick's appearance and behavior that he is in love. In the next instant the complacent vision of Claudio and Don Pedro is to be tested by the deceptions of Don John.

Just as the gentlemen have a scene devoted to the imagery of fashion and its meaning, the ladies also have their scene, in which, though the controlling theme of the play is less overt, it is still suggestively present: the "fine, quaint, graceful, and excellent fashion" of Hero's gown (Act III, Scene 4, 13-23), worth ten of any glittering show such as that of the Duchess of Milan's gown, may perhaps be taken to represent the reality of Hero herself. Beatrice herself appears in a new guise in this scene. Does Shakespeare mean to suggest further that Beatrice's new fashion, that of her quaintly dissembled love for Benedick, is worth ten of her glittering earlier guise as my Lady Disdain?

In the light of this emphasis on fashion in the imagery, it is interesting that the word *fashion* itself is employed in key incidents as a verb meaning to *shape* or *contrive* events (Act II, Scene 1, 384; Act II, Scene 2, 47; Act IV, Scene 1, 236). And it is in this sense of contriving or shaping the appearance of things that the most significant use of fashion occurs in this play. What was a set of images suddenly takes shape as a symbol, a personification of the theme, a creature who may be regarded as the shaper and contriver of the tangled web of appearances that composes the fabric of this play.

James A.S. McPeek

Dogberry and his fellows, from time to time the victims of

syllables like Mrs. Malaprop, are more frequently and more significantly, like the second Mrs. Quickly, the victims of ideas. When Verges speaks of "suffering salvation body and soul," and Dogberry of being "condemned into everlasting redemption," it is impossible they are being deceived merely by similitude of sounds. Rather, they are being confounded by ideas with which, though unfitted to do so, they feel it incumbent upon themselves to cope. Such utterances are of a piece with Dogberry's method of counting; with his preposterous examination of Conrade and Borachio, in which condemnation precedes questioning; with his farewell of Leonato, to whom, in an endeavour to conserve both their dignities, he "humbly gives leave to depart"; with his desire "to be written down an ass," in which the same sense of his own dignity is in conflict with, among other things, a sense that it needs vindication. It is not Mrs. Malaprop, but rather Bottom, who comes to mind here: Bottom who, like Dogberry, is torn between conflicting impulses — whether those of producing his interlude in as splendid a manner as possible, while at the same time showing as much deference as possible to the ladies; or of claiming as his own the "most rare vision" which, as a vision, certainly had been his, while for its rarity it seemed such as could not rightly belong to any man.

In thus addressing themselves to intellectual or moral feats of which they are not capable, Bottom, Mrs. Quickly and Dogberry do of course display a form of pride. Given his attitude towards Verges:

> a good old man, sir, he will be talking as they say, when the age is in, the wit is out, God helpe us, it is a world to see....

Dogberry's pride needs no stressing. It is however no longer a foolish pride; or if foolish, then not with the folly of Mrs. Malaprop, but rather of all the protagonists of drama, comic or tragic, who measure themselves against tasks which ultimately prove too much for them. Perhaps with justice it is to be classified as a form of *hybris*, a comic *hybris*; and if so, then some kind of essential relation between the Dogberry scenes and the tragically inclined scenes of the main plot is immediately suggested.

James Smith

It is here [in the church scene] that the social abnormality of aristocratic society in Messina is exposed once and for all for what it is — shallow and perverse application of a standard of behavior that is both automatic and uncharitable. In part, critical misunderstanding of this scene has sprung from failure to realize that the deception by Don John and Borachio of Claudio and Don Pedro into the belief that Hero is sexually loose is symbolic as well as psychological. Inability to see clearly at night is a common human trait, but in Claudio and Don

Pedro it symbolizes the dominant trait of aristocratic folk in Messina, in whom failure of physical eyesight is equivalent to moral confusion. Those who marry according to the philosophy of *caveat emptor*, like Claudio, are bound to be predisposed to sexual distrust, while their depreciation of love and marriage to the level of the market-place inevitably leads them to believe in virginity as the principal attribute of a bride-to-be.

Claudio's determination to expose Hero in church is quite in line with the social usage of his society, which accepted as legitimate harsh reprisal for sexual fraud, but he also exposes his general moral blindness. And the immediate compliance of Don Pedro (Act III, Scene 2, 126-130) indicates that Claudio's decision, however lacking in Christian charity, should not be reckoned a complete social abnormality. All those who reject Hero, even Leonato, assume they are justified, and they all behave melodramatically, just as shallow human beings are always inclined to thunder for justice in a social crisis when wounded pride, far more than moral shock, begins to stem up their ethical consciousness.

Nevertheless, Claudio's self-righteousness exposes a serious flaw in the social code: the superficiality of a value system that mistakes sexual purity for love is shown up in all its heartless folly. At the same time, the concurrent movement away from superficiality in Beatrice and Benedick, already under way, suggests how witlessness can be exchanged for wisdom. Stupidity versus intelligence is the underlying theme of the church scene and is dramatized by means of a typical Shakespearian problem in epistemology: under what conditions can the senses be trusted to provide accurate data for substantive knowledge of human character? To what degree do objective and subjective ways of knowing lead to rock-bottom truth about people we think we are familiar with?

Walter N. King

Much Ado About Nothing, as already suggested, is Shakespeare's nearest approach to the comedy of manners: the wit-combat between its predestinate lovers, besides being a favourite device of the author for establishing a lively familiarity between the parties, commits him to what is, in effect, the stock situation in a type of play which Congreve brought to perfection a century later. Beatrice and Benedick bickering their way into matrimony, are quite obviously assuming for our pleasure a social attitude which we know to be at variance with their true feelings and with the destiny which awaits them at the close.

In the pure comedy of manners as practised by Congreve sentiment or passion is conveyed by means of elegant understatement or downright contradiction...

The real point of the joke is that man is pretending to be civilised.

This is the stock situation of the comedy of manner. The elaborate ritual of society is a mask through which the natural man is comically seen to look....In the comedy of manners men and women are seen holding reality away, or letting it appear only as an unruffled thing of attitudes. Life is here made up of exquisite demeanour. Its comedy grows from the incongruity of human passion with its cool, dispassionate and studied expression. It ripples forth in ironic contemplation of people born to passion high and low, posing in the social mirror. This is the real justification of the term "artificial comedy" as applied to the plays of Congreve. We are born naked into nature. In the comedies of Congreve we are born again into civilisation and clothes. We are no longer men; we are wits and a peruke. We are no longer women; we are ladies of the tea-table. Life is absurdly mocked as a series of pretty attitudes and sayings. Hate is absurdly mirrored in agreeably bitter scandal. Perplexity and wonder are seen distorted in the mechanical turns of a swift and complicated plot. Always the fun lies in a sharp contrast between man civilised and the genial primitive creature peeping through.

. . .

Congreve wrote the undiluted comedy of manners, distilling pure water from the living spring. His characters must sustain to the end their manifest pretences that they have no feeling deeper than an epigram may carry; no aspiration higher than a fine coat may express; no impulse stronger than a smile may cover; no joy more thrilling than a nod may contain; no sorrow deeper than a pretty oath may convey. Shakespeare's comedy, on the other hand, consists in elaborating these pretences in order that they may at the right moment be effectively exploded. Beatrice and Benedick, who begin by seeming least likely of any in Messina to betray a genuine emotion, must in the end uncover their hearts.

John Palmer

Much Ado is a play of action springing from character, but it is also a play of vivacious and amusing dialogue. In fact a great part of the fun of this play comes from the spoken word; often, indeed, the action halts while we listen to a rippling stream of speech. The text falls easily into verse and prose; easily but not equally, for about three-fourths of the whole is in prose, a new phenomenon in Shakespearean comedy. Shakespeare's rustics and clownish servants, indeed, had talked in prose; a merry gentleman like Mercutio might step from verse into prose and back again. Here for the first time, however, the dialogue of gentlefolk, male and female, is for the most part couched in prose. It seems as if Shakespeare is now convinced that for comedy of the lighter, less romantic type, prose is the proper vehicle. The conviction may have grown on him while he was creating Falstaff, his greatest comic figure, who seldom speaks a line of verse. The conjecture seems to be confirmed by the fact that King Henry's wooing of his French bride, perhaps the least romantic courtship in English drama, is all in prose. This scene is plainly meant to round off a drum-and-trumpet play with a concluding strain of comedy, and *King Henry V* was written in the same year as *Much Ado*.

Little need be said of the verse of this play. There are good lines here and there, but there is an absence alike of the lyric music of the *Dream* and the grave eloquence of *The Merchant*. The workmanlike verse is confined almost without exception, to what is structurally the main, which is also the derived, plot, another proof, no doubt, of Shakespeare's slight regard for this action compared with his delight in the new theme and the two characters that he was adding to it. It is the prose and not the poetry of this play that lingers in the memory: the comic blunders of Dogberry, the wit-combats of the still defiant lovers, the scoffing comments of Benedick on love and marriage, the light-hearted jesting of Beatrice, and, best of all, the confession of their mutual love in simple unadorned prose. It was from Lyly, no doubt, that Shakespeare learned the use of prose in comedy, but he had by this time happily purged his style of the characteristic marks of Lylian Euphuism.

Thomas Marc Parrott

Benedick and Beatrice in *Much Ado* are...mechanical comic humors, prisoners of their own wit, until a benevolent practical joke enables their real feelings to break free of their verbal straitjackets. This benevolent practical joke is in contrast to the malevolent one that Don John plays on Claudio, which, though far more painful in its effects, operates according to the same comic laws. Claudio becomes engaged to Hero without also engaging his loyalty: he retains the desire to be rid of her if there should be any inconvenience in the arrangement, and this desire acts precisely like a humor, blinding him to the obvious facts of his situation. In his second marriage ceremony he pledges his loyalty first, before he has seen the bride, and this releases him from his humorous bondage.

Northrop Frye

Shakespeare's plays, says Meredith, are saturated with the golden light of comedy — the comedy that is redemptive as tragedy cannot be. Consider what happens in *Much Ado About Nothing* when Benedick makes the startling comic discovery that he himself, together with the other mistaken people in the play, is a fool. Here is a moral perception that competes with tragic "recognition." The irony of Benedick's "recognition" is searching, for he has boasted, all along, that he cannot find it in his heart to love any of Eve's daughters, least of all Beatrice. And Beatrice, for her part, has avowed she will never be fitted with a husband until God makes men of some other metal than earth. Both these characters are too deep of draught to sail in the shoal waters of sentimentality, and both have bravely laid a course of their own far outside the matchmaking that goes easily on in Messina. Each is a mocker, or eiron; but in being so, each becomes the boaster (alazon) betrayed into the valiant pose that they are exempt from love. Then they both walk, wide-eyed, like "proud" Oedipus, into the trap they have laid for themselves. There they see themselves as they are. When Benedick hears himself called hard-hearted he suffers the bewilderment of comic discovery and knows that his pose as mocker is no longer tenable. So he turns his scornful eye inward upon his own vanity: if Beatrice is sick for love of his ribald self he must give up his misogyny and get him a wife. He yields himself, absurdly, to Beatrice, saying "Happy are they that hear their detractions and can put them to mending." At the extreme of his own shame Benedick is compelled to see himself as he sees others, together along a low horizon. Thus occur the comic purgation, the comic resignation to the human lot, the comic humbling of the proud, the comic ennobling after an act of blindness. Those who play a comic role, like Benedick or Berowne or Meredith's Sir Willoughby Patterne, wrongheadedly are liable to achieve their own defeat and afterwards must hide their scars. The comic and the tragic heroes alike "learn through suffering," albeit suffering in comedy takes the form of humiliation, disappointment, or chagrin, instead of death.

Wylie Sypher

Bibliography

Barber, C.L. *Shakespeare's Festive Comedy*. Princeton, N.J.: Princeton University Press, 1959.

Bradbrook, M.C. *The Growth and Structure of Elizabethan Comedy*. London: Chatto and Windus, 1955.

Brown, John Russell. *Shakespeare and His Comedies*. London: Hillary House Publishers Ltd., 1957.

Bullough, Geoffrey, ed. *Comedies, 1597-1603*. New York: Columbia University Press, 1958.

Chambers, Edmund K. *William Shakespeare: A Study of Facts and Problems*. 2 Vols. New York: Oxford University Press, 1930.

Charlton, H.B. *Shakespearian Comedy*. New York: Barnes & Noble, 1963.

Clemen, Wolfgang H. *The Development of Shakespeare's Imagery*. Cambridge, Mass.: Harvard University Press, 1951.

Evans, Bertrand. *Shakespeare's Comedy*. Oxford: Oxford University Press at the Clarendon Press, 1960.

Gordon, George. *Shakespearean Comedy*. Oxford: Oxford University at the Clarendon Press, 1944.

Meader, William G. *Courtship in Shakespeare, Its Relation to the Tradition of Courtly Love*. New York: King's Crown Press, 1954.

Muir, Kenneth. *Shakespeare's Sources: Comedies and Tragedies*. London: Methuen & Co., 1957.

Palmer, John. *Comic Characters of Shakespeare*. London: The Macmillan Company, 1946.

Parrott, Thomas M. *Shakespearean Comedy*. New York: Russell & Russell, 1949.

Partridge, Eric. *Shakespeare's Bawdy*. New York: E.P. Dutton & Co., 1955.

Pettet, E.C. *Shakespeare and the Romance Tradition*. London: Staples Press, 1949.

Phialas, Peter G. *Shakespeare's Romantic Comedies*. Chapel Hill: University of North Carolina Press, 1966.

Prouty, Charles T. *The Sources of "Much Ado About Nothing."* New Haven: Yale University Press, 1950.

Richmond, Hugh M. *Shakespeare's Sexual Comedy: A Mirror for Lovers*. New York: Bobbs-Merrill, Inc., 1971.

Salingar, Leo. *Shakespeare and the Traditions of Comedy*. London: Cambridge University Press, 1974.

Swinden, Patrick. *An Introduction to Shakespeare's Comedies*. London: Macmillan, 1973.

Wilson, J. Dover. *Shakespeare's Happy Comedies*. London: Faber and Faber, 1962.